ON PLAYING
THE BACK NINE

BY
WILLIAM A. RITTER

On Playing The Back Nine

Copyright © 2018 by (William A. Ritter)

ISBN-13: 978-1983606915
ISBN-10: 198360691X

Acknowledgements

It was Margret Mead who popularized the opinion that it takes a village to raise a child. Which is surely true. But as for me, I am more interested in whether it takes a church to raise a preacher. Because, in my case, that's what happened. Was it something in the air there? Possibly. Was it something in the leadership there? Occasionally. Or was it something in the congregation there? Most assuredly.

The church was Westlawn Methodist Church in Detroit. It flourished in the mid-1900s before dying a quiet death in 1977. I wrote about its influence in a previously published reflection entitled, "Connecting the Dots." But now, to the small remnant who are left, scattered though they may be, again I say, "Thank you."

To my professors at Albion College (1958-1962) and Yale Divinity School (1962-1965) who fueled and fired my mind while smelting and refining my material, I also say, "Thank you."

To a quartet of professional models (Bill Muehl, Fred Buechner, Gene Lowry, and Fred Craddock) who left an indelible imprint on my preaching style, I say, "Hopefully, I wore it well."

To the members of some wonderful congregations, who took me in, heard me out, cheered me on, and prayed me up, words of thanks hardly seem enough.

To people like Janet Smylie who, for over twenty-five years, put words on a page so they were both legible and grammatical, I couldn't have done it without you.

To Katelyn Drake who, along with Ann and Zeno Windley, provided photographic support for these pages, I express my appreciation. If pictures really do trump words in bringing home a message, you have given this book a wonderful advantage.

To Lindsay Hinz, whose way with words often exceeds my own, and whose knowledge of advertising, marketing, publishing, and, on most days, Christianity, assists me in my movement from wordsmith to communicator, her gracious and beautifully-written forward is proof of everything I have just said. I sometimes find myself asking, "How did I ever discover or deserve such a collaborator?"

To my wife, Kristine, who has helped me understand and express what is inside me, by spending over fifty years walking beside me, I owe everything.

And to my daughter, Julie Hopkins, who continually proves that any bread I cast upon her waters always comes back to me as cake, I dedicate this book. The flavoring she has brought to her mother and me continues to sweeten our lives beyond measure.

TABLE OF CONTENTS

FOREWORD

I've read a bunch of books. And sermons. And other stuff that ministers and pastors and theologians and really good writers have written. You know, the stuff that makes you think, think really hard, about how this life we're all unfolding relates to the faith we're all trying to define. I've read the old and the new books, the blogs and chapters and musings on scripture as they relate to our harsh, in-your-face, modern-day realities, and the struggle we all seem to have when trying to make them mesh. It seems there are chapters in every kind of book that can make any of us nod in agreement, laugh out loud, question how the preacher got so inside our head, or bring even the most stoic of readers to tears.

I've also read dozens of Bill Ritter's sermons. I've heard Bill preach even more of Bill's sermons. And I fall into that portion of his fan base that hears him; no, I mean, actually, almost distractingly, brings him and his voice and his pulpit styling along for the read inside our heads. If you're in that group, you understand. If not, it may not matter. I figure whether you know that voice, that skilled delivery, that masterful weaving of human nature and scriptural wisdom, or not, you deserve to be warned.

Before you settle in your favorite spot at home, before you smooth the beach towel out and fold back the book cover, or prior to tucking these chapters in a bag you're about to carry onto an airplane, be aware. In short, I wish you good luck getting through this one without a gulp or two. And I mean that in the best way imaginable.

If you're cracking the spine on this book, I think it's safe to assume you've been to church. That, in turn, means you've experienced a dry or boring or even offensive sermon or two. You've found yourself listening to a less-than-tantalizing orator, and wondered what escape route you could take, or tuned out completely while pondering your grocery list, or found yourself hoping that nobody saw you nearly drift off to sleep. But if you've ever been moved by a sermon, sat in church and wondered how God put you there so that the preacher standing in the pulpit could talk directly to you, all the time wondering why all these other people are surrounding you and listening in on your personal, private, telepathic connecting message from above, then you are destined to report that this book "speaks to you." Problem is, you're everybody. Good thing is, you're everybody. That's because everybody has experienced the sensation of scripture and story somehow blending to pack a punch. And the really good thing is, Ritter packs it better than most. In other words, bring your authentic self to this read. Bring honesty and humility. And maybe a tissue or two.

Now, like most people, I like things that "move" me. Ruffle my feathers. Open my memory banks. Soften my guard. But I've noticed that most uncomfortable or tender or "aha" experiences seem to come to you and me without us orchestrating them. Even when we go looking for them … in books or sermons or forums of any kind … they're evasive. I've determined that it's not a matter of what you like. Or what you choose. Or what you've been taught, that will deliver those stirring moments when life and faith mix to make the best impact on your heart. Those nourishing moments are a gift. Those provocative moments are a gift. Those letting it all in and letting it all out moments are a gift. When reading this collection, I think people will agree that they've been gifted with the artistry of one learned man bringing you a story or two that you were meant to hear. You will be convinced you are the only one he is talking to. And you may hunger for more, even though you will have been well fed.

Once you're done, you'll wish you could catch one of his appearances in a pulpit near you. But you can't. And you'll wonder if his website or any of the churches he has served will provide recordings of him sharing stuff like this so that you can discover what it is folks are talking about (or maybe just take an out loud trip down Memory Lane). But they won't. I predict that you'll want to share this book with all sorts of people that you know who may need to swallow the reminders that are on these pages. And you should. And I'll bet that you'll spend a fair amount of time after each chapter contemplating the way your life fills in the blanks that the story reveals. And that's good.

Mostly, it warms my heart to know that these words have been prepared for the sharing. I'm touched to call this man my dear, dear friend. And I'm happy to know that others will take him, and the wonderful teachings that are his ministry, into their heads and hearts.

Finding the grace in every day,

Lindsay Hinz

Bill has shared nearly twenty-five years of collaboration and friendship with Lindsay Hinz. They created their first stewardship campaign together in 1994.

Introduction

Kindly allow me to apologize at the outset for what will soon become obvious. This is not a book about golf. Those of you who have seen me play already know that, given that I am not a very good golfer. I have never played more than twenty rounds a year, never played enough rounds at any one course to establish a handicap, never scored in the eighties, never made it to the final round in any tournament, and have generally considered bogey golf (18 strokes over par) to be a wonderful score.

But I was a happy hacker, figuring that golf was a game you played with nice people, on nice days, in nice places. Those nice places included Old Prestwick in Scotland and Oakland Hills in Michigan. But my chief claim to fame involved getting eighteen fellow travelers on the Old Course in St. Andrews, the alleged birthplace of golf in Scotland.

Virtually every golfer who has heard my title *(On Playing The Back Nine)* has asked what I plan to say about the 19th hole. Which I know as a place to sip a little, munch a little, stretch the truth a little, while explaining how I coulda played better, shoulda played better, and certainly will play better the next time. As evidence that such improvement might actually be possible, I point to that marvelous pitch and putt on hole No. 17 … those two shots being the gifts of a gracious God who once decreed (somewhere in Leviticus) that all duffers and hackers ought to experience two or three shots each round, forever to be known as "the shots that bring you back."

No, this book is not about that game. For if it had been, I would have had to include a pair of my earlier sermons entitled, *On Playing In The Fairway* (which I didn't), and *When You Most Need A Mulligan* (which I did). This is why I found it hard to believe my parishioners when they told me how much religion they regularly experience on the golf course, which is simply the first lie that golfers tell each other at 11:00 o'clock on Sunday morning.

Enough already. Having read this far you know that my title, *"On Playing the Back Nine,"* is about the latter stages of life's journey. That's because the "back nine" is the finishing nine. If you are going to make a swing correction, it's now or never. If you are going to make a score improvement, it's now or never. If you are going to salvage or resurrect anything from this round, it's now or never. And the 'back nine" is also where it occurs to you that you are lucky that you're not carrying your own bag, given that caddies have made the journey walk-able or carts have made the course drive-able. Seeing people on the course who need neither caddies nor carts leads people like me to say, "there'll come a day," even as I ask them if they'd like to "play through."

When golfers read my title, virtually every one of them speculates as to where on the back nine they are presently located. Nobody thinks they are standing on the tenth tee. But most express hope that they are not putting on the eighteenth green. As for me, what do I know? I'd rather not render a projection. But I do sense that from where I presently stand, I can see the clubhouse without binoculars.

Truth be told, my original title had nothing to do with "nines," front or back. It had to do with rivers … biblical rivers … deep rivers … chilly rivers.

A hymn loved by many is entitled, *When the Storms Of Life Are Raging, Stand By Me (No. 512, United Methodist Hymnal).* Listen closely to verse five:

When I'm growing old and feeble, stand by me

When I'm growing old and feeble, stand by me

When my life becomes a burden,

And I'm nearing chilly Jordan,

O, thou lily of the valley,

Stand by me.

Which I know something about. I have been to the Jordan, have done several adult baptisms (by immersion) in the Jordan, and I know that where I have entered it, the Jordan is neither chilly nor cold. But for years, hymns and spirituals have labeled it as such, with lyrics linking the Jordan with dying. "Crossing over Jordan" is going to the other side. Countless are the sermons that have urged the dying to, "have no fear, since our Father owns the land on both sides of the river. " A talented preacher can spin that narrative into a funeral sermon that provides comfort for the family of the one who has crossed, or the individuals who have yet to. This is why my original title read, *When I'm Nearing Chilly Jordan,* for I am a preacher who has taken multiple groups to Israel, as well as being a preacher who loves to sing. Consider these familiar lyrics …

And then one day I'll cross that river,

I'll fight life's final war with pain.

Till my raptured soul shall find, rest beyond the river.

Michael, row your boat ashore. Alleluia.

River Jordan is chilly and cold … chills the body but not the soul.

When I tread the verge of Jordan,

Bid my anxious fears subside.

But as I field-tested my title with a wide audience of friends, I found that the image "Chilly Jordan" did not compute with many of them. And even those who knew the reference thought that marrying the word "chilly" to the word "Jordan" sounded like a downer. But virtually everybody resonated with the image of the "back nine." Not only could they understand it, they could visualize it. So now you know.

But why this book now? First, because others have published material on a similar theme ... I am talking about people who shared my profession, earned my admiration, and have lifespans of a common duration.

There is Fred Craddock who, when he was seventy-eight, wrote about his call to preach in a little book entitled, *Connecting the Dots*. Then there was Elton Trueblood, the great Quaker philosopher, and teacher, who did something similar when he was seventy-four, his title being, *While It Is Day*. And one certainly recalls the widely published preacher/novelist, Frederick Buechner, who first wrote about his own citing of "Chilly Jordan" when he was seventy-five. As I write, I am cruising toward my seventy-eighth birthday. Simply put, the time seems right.

Second, it is becoming clearer and clearer to me that while most careers have limits, so do the number of years when one can capably write about careers and limits. I love to write. People keep encouraging me to write. But as Maxie Dunham once wrote, "old Pappy Time is picking my pocket." So, when anybody asks why I am writing this book now, I simply answer, "because, I can." For more than fifty years, whatever else my employers got from me, they got an employee who was durable. During forty years of pulpit ministry, I never once missed a Sunday when I was expected to preach. During five years on the faculty of Duke Divinity School, I never once missed a class that I was expected to teach. And during six-and-a-half years as the Director of the United Methodist Union of Greater Detroit, I never once missed a board meeting that I was expected to lead. And then there were twenty months of Interim Assignments where I showed up on time, every time, to do what was needed at the time.

I can't say that anymore. Nor can I do that anymore. My mind is still clear and my voice resonant. But my pace is slowing and my gait is faltering. Four years ago, the doctors at the University of Michigan Adult Neurology Center said, "You have some kind of motor neuron disease but we can't exactly define what it is." My doctor, Eva Feldman, is world famous and her research specialty is ALS (more commonly known as Lou Gehrig's Disease). Which is what I first thought I had. Thankfully, they are now walking back that opinion, but have yet to give me a replacement title. Whatever I have is progressive. But, for the time being, things are stable. Which further explains my phrase, "because, I can."

This is a book of sermons (twenty-one to be exact) covering approximately twenty years. I liked them when I wrote them. And others seemed to like them when they heard them. Are they the best things I've ever done? Not necessarily. But they're honest, carefully crafted, and they fit my theme.

So, what is my theme? Let me state it as simply as I can ...

As I traverse the latter years of my journey, I find myself wanting to share glimpses of ...

> ... a philosophy that explains me

> ... a faith that sustains me

> ... and a view of life's end that inspires confidence within me

As I said earlier, these are sermons. They were written to be heard, not read. Nothing has changed. They are still written to be heard. But I am confident that you will be able to hear between the lines.

Feel free to approach this book any way you like. These sermons were not preached sequentially, so why would you feel constrained to read them sequentially? I have been amazed by the number of readers of my last book who told me that they read one sermon a day, somewhat akin to a daily devotional. While another reader said she read it from beginning to end two times in a row. You will find a lot of me in these sermons, although this collection is neither an autobiography, nor a memoir. But on my better days in the pulpit, the material and the messenger became hard to separate. And on my very best days, my listeners became one with both the content and the preacher, creating a trinity of connectivity. Philosophers used to ask if a tree fell in the forest and there was no one there to hear it, did it actually make a noise? I suppose the same question could be asked of a sermon. Without someone like you, dear friend, to read it or hear it, did it ever really happen? And even if it did, did it really matter?

*Left to right, Julie Hopkins, Georgia Hopkins, Jared Hopkins,,
Kris Ritter, Bill Ritter, Jacob Hopkins floating along at Aulani
Resort (Disney) Honolulu, Hawaii, 2017*

When you read this book, I pray that it will continue to happen. And maybe, just maybe, it will matter greatly. But in concluding these reflections, I invite you to hear the closing lines of Ervin Drake's lovely ballad, *It Was a Very Good Year.*

But now the days draw short

I'm in the autumn of my years

And I think of my life as vintage wine

From fine old kegs

From the brim to the dregs

(When) poured sweet and clear

It was a very good year.

Strange verb, "poured." Some of my professional colleagues associate it with the outpouring of the Holy Spirit. Others, with the sacramental outpouring of the blood of Christ. But whether you thirst for something from Calvary or something from California, pull up a chair … pass your glass … and let us drink together.

Bill Ritter

September 2018

Note: The song, It Was A Very Good Year, was written by Irvin Drake in 1961 and subsequently recorded by Frank Sinatra. The "outpouring of the Holy Spirit" is first spoken by the prophet, Joel, and reprised in Acts 2: 17. The outpouring of the blood of Calvary is language found in the United Methodist Communion Liturgy.

1

DRAGGING OUR TALES BEHIND US

When referring to my preaching, people often interchange the word 'sermon" with the word "story." "I love your stories," they say. "They are so incredibly illuminating about life," they continue. While I sense they are saying something complimentary, I worried, early on, that I might be doing something wrong. This sermon, preached near the end of my twelve years in Birmingham, addresses such worries. Stories not only illuminate, but stories connect. I once heard several members of a large congregation lament that, "Nobody here knows my story." And that congregation employed not one, not two, but three pastors.

Scripture: Psalm 137: 1-6

Several years ago, a member of this church for whom I have enormous respect walked into my office, shut the door, took a seat, and shared his reason for coming to see me. "I know we know each other," he said. "But given my lack of family to tell my story when the time comes, I wanted to tell you a little bit more about myself. Because the chances are pretty good that I am going to die on your watch."

Well, he was wrong (or so it would seem). Time is running out on "my watch" faster than it is running out on his life. Which reminds me of the day, early in my ministry, when a family invited me to sit down at their dining room table and take copious notes about their grandfather ("So as to get this little matter out of the way before Grandpa dies, and things get hectic.") Several years later I moved from the area, and among the things I threw away were those notes for grandpa's eulogy. Unused.

Funny word, "eulogy." We don't use it much anymore. And few are those who understand it anymore. Once upon a time, it betokened a speech at a funeral … often delivered by clergy. But not always. Sometimes a relative eulogized the dead. Or a coworker. Or a friend. Maybe all three (with clergy batting cleanup).

A eulogy is both personal and biographical … usually laudatory. It comes in the form of a tribute, often hitting the high spots while circumventing the low ones. Though not always. I've heard people go to the podium, adjust the microphone, and talk about what a scoundrel old Harry was. But usually with a twinkle in the eye. And never, so far as I could tell, with malicious intent.

To this day, people ask me to deliver eulogies. Or they ask me "if I'd be willing to say a few words." In fact, the question is put to me in those terms more often than any other. Less often am I asked to "deliver a sermon" at someone's funeral. "Sermon" being a word for insiders. "Eulogy" being a word for outsiders. Is there a distinction in popular culture? I think there is. The word "sermon" is most often associated with the proclamation of the Gospel. The word "eulogy" is more often associated with the personalization of a life. Unless, of course, one does both ... mix biography and theology in the same message. Which is what I do. And always have. If I preach your funeral, I'll talk about your life. But I will also talk about the Lord and his promises.

Though not everybody will. The very first funeral I ever attended was for my Great Aunt Emma. And if I hadn't known I was in the right room (which I discerned because my father was on one side of me and my mother was on the other side of me), nothing her German Lutheran pastor said would have clued me in. Given that he didn't say anything about Emma. He said a lot about the Lord (who, as I recall, was portrayed in terms more frightening than comforting ... but hey, what did I know? I was just a kid.) But he said nothing about Emma. He did repeat her name in the prayer ... mispronouncing it, as I recall (he couldn't quite get his tongue wrapped around Michefske). But I don't think he knew her. Although I did recall Aunt Emma and Uncle John once taking me to a sauerkraut supper at his church. Which I hated (the sauerkraut, not the church). But I am sure he was taught in seminary that the purpose of a funeral sermon is to glorify God and that too much detail about any human life ... even a very good human life ... is too much like glorifying man and, therefore, dangerously close to that slippery slope called idolatry.

To this day, I go to funerals where the preacher will group

personal remarks (presenting them at one point in the service), only to return later in the service with religious remarks … as if to suggest that putting them together in the same message might inappropriately mix things human with things divine. The inference being that things human are not worthy of being coupled with things divine.

Yet each of us has a story. And each story is significant. When we die, our story ought to be remembered as best as it can be remembered. And it ought to be told as best as it can be told. It ought to be told honestly. It ought not be airbrushed or cosmeticized. People who knew the deceased should recognize the person they knew in the words I share. Which leads my critics to ask, "What if there were things about the deceased that were less the decorous … addictions not completely conquered … temptations not completely avoided … battles not completely won?" Well, if everybody knows those things, there's no point in avoiding them. But I can talk about how hard the struggle was and how, from time to time, the individual wrestled with it.

One of my favorite lines comes from the pen of the late Mary Jane Irion. Who, as the time of her dying drew near, said to her pastor, "Tell my friends to remember that the good I did in life did not have to be perfect to be effective … and that something of who I was will go on lending aid in this amazing human endeavor."

Worse come to worst, I could probably say the same about you. But when the time comes, how will I tell your story if I do not know your story? I once had one of you approach me in Fellowship Hall following a funeral and say, " I can't wait to die and hear what you're going to say about me." Unfortunately, I didn't know all that much to say about her. But when the time comes, her family will tell me. As will her friends. I even invited her to drop by the office and give me the scoop (at least as she saw it).

In planning a service, one of the best things I do is sit down with as large a group of survivors as I can gather. I ask a few questions. I stimulate a good conversation. Then I take careful notes. Families always approach such moments reluctantly. But everybody leaves the experience gratefully. They find such conversations helpful. We start with bare facts. Then we share stories. One story speaks to another … complete with lots of tears, but more than a little laughter. And now that I've been here a while, I've got many of you trained. To whatever degree you know something about the deceased that I might be able to use, you call me and tell me. My job is to gather it in and tell it well.

Each story is important. Why? Because God loves us in our particularity, that's why. How many times have you heard me say, "Each of us is a unique, unrepeatable miracle of creation"? Which means I should eulogize you in your uniqueness. At the moment of your departing, it is not my job to evaluate your life, but to give thanks for it.

Although if that's all I did, I would be shortchanging you. For your story is set within the context of a greater story. God's story. Meaning that when death closes your chapter (long or short), the one thing death cannot do is wrench the pen from the Author of Life. Meaning that there is more to be written. And more that will be written. Which is both a promise offered by me and a mystery that is beyond me. So, I articulate it with caution and passion. Yet when people comment on my funeral sermons, they are more likely to focus on the part that was personal than on the part that was theological.

In those conversations, a funny thing happens. You who knew the deceased well will often say to me, "Thanks to you, I learned a lot of things about Harry that I never knew before." And I find myself wondering, "If you knew Harry for thirty years and I put this together in an hour and a half, how can that be?" Unless Harry didn't share all that much. Or you didn't listen all that well.

In a world where teenagers now put their deepest thoughts into online journals (for the uninitiated, they're called "blogs"), I think there is both a hunger to share and a fear of sharing. When Lynn Hasley preached her first sermon this summer, she talked about the value of persons and the importance of stories. In reality, she was making an appeal. New, as she was … green, as she was … strange, as she was … Lynn was saying, "I'll give you a part of me if you'll trust me with a part of you. And a church ought to be the place where that can happen. "

Well, Damian Zikakis … my favorite Greek (who has lived a wonderful story and who tells other wonderful stories) … came up to Lynn and said, "I hear you. I'm with you. Let's get together and brainstorm what kinds of ministries we could develop that involve story telling." And they've come a long way since that sermon. Better yet, they are close to going public with that ministry. I don't know what form it will take. But it could be wonderful. I mean, why should we wait till we die to have someone discover who we were?

Although no story is just about us. Every story is full of other people who have journeyed with us. And full of the God who has journeyed with us ... perceived or unperceived.

I love Psalm 137 because it is so wonderfully honest and gut-wrenchingly human. It is about the people of Israel. But, at the time of the writing, they are not in Israel. They are in Babylon (Iraq). They have been exiled there ... a forced deportation, if you will. And they do not have the faintest idea when, if ever, they are going to get back.

Once they were singing people. Now they are weeping people. Where are their instruments, you ask? Hanging in the trees, that's where they are. But it gets worse. The people who have captured them are making sport of them, saying (in effect):

> You guys sang once.
>> We don't hear you singing now.
> What's up with that?
>> Let's have a little music.
>>> Sing, you stupid slaves.
>>> Sing! Sing!

Well, they have a defense. They sang when they were the home team. Now they're the away team. "We can't sing when we are the away team," they say. "No way can we sing when we're the away team."

But then, one of their own says, "Oh, but we have to. Sing, that is. Because if we don't sing of the days that were, we'll never survive the days that are. We don't know what's going on now … how it's going to turn out now … whether we're going to live or die now … or where in hell God is now. But if we don't sing the songs and tell the stories of a time and place when we knew the answers to those questions, we're gonna shrivel up and die now."

I can't remember who said it. But years ago I heard a wonderful definition of a friend …

A friend is someone who knows your song so well,
that they can sing it back to you when you've
forgotten the lyrics and can only remember a few
snatches of the tune.

And all of us should have such a friend. Heck, all of us should be such a friend. But our odds increase when people take the time to nurture that level of friendship.

A colleague of mine, ministering to a very poor community in Detroit, recently asked a group of women what they would do if they won the Lottery? "What would I do if I won the Lottery?" one woman said. "I'd buy easy chairs for the laundromat, enough chairs so that everybody could sit down and take a load off. All they've got there is three old chairs including two with broken seats. And the one that's not broken is so hard you'd rather sit on a dryer and burn your ---. You know what I mean, pastor."

The pastor pressed the point, asking if there wasn't anything else she would want to do with the money. "No," she said. "Just chairs for the laundromat."

So let me ask you. Assuming she buys them, where do you think she will place them? Do you see them scattered … one here … one there … another by the soap dispenser? Set apart? Separate? Singular? Or do you see them together?

I see them together. So folks can talk to each other. Because not all the laundry that people bring to such places can be squeezed into those machines and washed clean in just forty minutes.

October 17, 2004
First United Methodist Church
Birmingham, Michigan

Note: *As concerns the 137th Psalm, I have preached it before. I first became acquainted with its phrases at Albion College, thanks to a moving choral anthem, "By The Rivers of Babylon," by Professor Anthony Taffs. Purists will note that I said nothing about the verses 7-9, which are among the most vengeful lines printed in Holy Scripture. These are the lines that conclude: "Happy shall be he who takes your little ones and dashes them against the rock." Obviously, the psalmist is willing to "let it all hang out," feeling no need to conceal the raw edge of human emotion from the reader. As I said in the sermon, Psalm 137 is gut-wrenchingly honest. I did not say that it is pretty. Having spoken of such things before, I feel no need to plow that ground again.*

The words of Mary Jane Irion first surfaced in a devotional book entitled, Soundings, by Rev. Dr. Robert Raines.

The story about chairs for the Laundromat has been widely told by the Rev. Dr. Faith Fowler, who included portions of it in her recent book, This Far By Faith.

Bill and Kris on a Chinese junk in Victoria Harbor, Hong Kong celebrating Kris's 65th birthday.

2

A TALE OF TWO POCKETS

I have long loved the imagery of this ancient Jewish narrative, especially when coupled with a most imaginative story by a Roman Catholic monk. So, I framed it in a pair of paradoxical texts from the Old Testament and preached it to a New Testament congregation. Enjoy.

Scripture: Genesis 3: 17-19, Psalms 8: 1-5

Several years ago I shared with you an ancient piece of rabbinic wisdom, often referred to as *"The Tale of Two Pockets."* Without testing the memory of the house, I will share its essence once again.

It is said that a pair of pants has two pockets for the purpose of carrying two messages. The messages speak to a pair of moods, equally powerful, equally distinct from the other, yet equally capable of dominating one's personality. The first of the moods is pride. The second, despair. The pockets carry a message for each.

The proud man, you may remember, is encouraged to reach into his left pocket, withdraw a piece of paper, unfold it at the point of its well-worn creases and read, " **Remember, you are dust and ashes.**" The words are an antidote to those who are riding high.

The despairing man is encouraged to reach into his right pocket, withdrawing a similarly-folded piece of paper, whereupon is to be found the reminder: "**For you, the entire universe was created.**" These words supply the antidote to those who are feeling low.

I don't know about you, but I continue to insist that all my trousers come with dual pockets. I need both reminders and find myself in the habit of reading them regularly. My friend, Carl Price, once included a prayer of invocation in his worship bulletin, which began thusly …

> O Lord, meet us this morning at the point
> of our various needs,
> known and unknown, expressed and denied.
> Some of us are high and need the humbling word.
> Some of us are low and need the lifting word.

His implication, of course, was that the worship service ought to provide both words, one to be heard by those who are soaring, the other to be heard by those who are sinking.

I don't know whether you are soaring or sinking this morning, but just as my pants pockets carry a word for either extreme, so (too) will this sermon carry an extension of those admonitions, in the hopes that the high will be humbled and the low will be exalted.

Let's draw from the left pocket first. "Remember, Ritter; you are dust and ashes." It is a message I need to hear. It says that I am both fallible and finite. It says that I am deadly and dying. It says that I don't amount to much. It also says that I won't last very long. And it says that all of the above are part and parcel of being human. It is a word that comes from the earliest mythic story of our origins.

God creates a garden and sets the terms of its occupancy. Man rebels, rejects the terms, and is denied occupancy. The story closes with a trinity of curses, delivered by God and levied upon the serpent, the woman, and the man. God closes His speech with the following words to Adam:

> "With sweat on your brow, you shall eat your bread,
> until you return to the soil as you were taken from it.
> For dust you are, and to dust you shall return."

Concerning that judgment, Dr. John Gibson of the University of Edinburgh adds:

> It is a fitting end, for dust is where men and women belong. Their abilities, their achievements, their wisdom, their acknowledgments, their insights, their technologies, their knowledge … none of these things entitles them to anything better. Everything these

dust-rooted creatures touches turns to ashes. Yet they still play God and delude themselves into promising Paradise for everybody, if not today, at least by tomorrow. But for all their promises, they cannot deliver the goods.

That's heavy stuff. But it is not without truth. We are dust and ashes. We are not much. We are not for long. Like grass, we have our day of greening and growing in the sun. But when it is no longer day, we wither … we fade … we are cut down … and we are thrown on the pile for burning.

Only twice do the words "dust and ashes" appear together in scripture (Genesis 18: 27 and Job 30:19). And, in both cases, the words are not a judgment voiced by God, so much as they are a testimony voiced, autobiographically, by man. This self-application is made first by Abraham, and, subsequently, by Job. Each announces, "I am dust and ashes." Suppose I were to follow suit and head for the Samaritan Counseling Center. Upon being asked for a brief description of my problem, what if I were to reply, "I am dust and ashes." Wes Brun would immediately begin to treat me for low self-esteem and a negative self-image. And he would be right. But so, too, would I. Be right, that is. I am dust and ashes. I am not much. I am not for long. That is my nature. That is also a biblical appraisal.

The Bible, you see, in its own inimitable way, often speaks a humbling word. It constrains and, occasionally, deflates my ego. It causes me to question my significance. It reminds me that I am not all that important. My colleague, Barry Johnson, writes, "Yes, we are children of God. Yes, we are joint heirs of Christ. Yes, we are unique, unrepeatable miracles of creation. Yes, we are gifted and blessed, each in our own way. And, yes, we are equipped by God to handle life's challenges and graced by God at the point of our failures. But in spite of all these attributes, there is not one of us without whom life would not go on. And no one of us is so important that the rest of the world should adjust itself to us."

Anthony de Mello tells a wonderful story about a flea who decided one day to move his family into an elephant's ear. Not wanting to appear presumptuous, the flea climbed up on the great behemoth, cupped his hands to his mouth and shouted:

> "Mr. Elephant, my family and I are particularly attracted to your ear. It looks precisely like the kind of neighborhood we have been looking for, and we would like to move in next week. We do have two children. But they are both well-behaved, and neither owns a moped. We can supply references and will consider any responsible security deposit. Therefore, if you have any objections to this proposal, kindly let me know by Friday so that I can make other arrangements. "

Hearing nothing from the elephant, who was completely oblivious to his presence, the flea and his family moved in the following Monday. They had been living there for only a week or two, when the flea's wife came home and announced, " I've just been visiting my cousin who lives down in Hoof Hollow. I like that neighborhood even better than ours. Can we move?" Once more the master of the house approached the elephant, cupped his hands around his mouth and shouted:

"Mr. Elephant, sir, I'm sorry to be such a bother, but my wife just located a long-lost cousin living in your hoof. It seems that they haven't seen each other in years. I suppose you know how that goes. Now, she wants to move. So, if it's all right with you, we'll surrender our security deposit and call somebody to clean the carpets. If I hear nothing to the contrary by Tuesday, we'll be relocating to your hoof by the first of next week."

Again, the elephant did not reply. So, the fleas packed up and moved. To which de Mello observes, "Relax! The universe doesn't even know you exist!"

While still pondering the author's conclusion, I do love his story. It does wonders in addressing our sometimes grandiose and exalted preoccupation with self. The universe does not begin and end with us. Neither does the world turn for the primary purpose of doing our bidding. If this contributes to an occasional feeling of insignificance, so be it. It ought to. I would even submit, for your consideration, that occasional feelings of insignificance are not entirely bad feelings to have. Some of us do tend to take ourselves too seriously. We need a word that notches us down a peg. We also need permission to relax.

Among those who might perceive a word about man's insignificance as being good news are a couple of groups, namely, those who suffer from a "center stage complex" and those who suffer from a "Messiah complex." Let's look at each group in turn. The center stage phobics fear the spotlight. But their initial mistake is in assuming the spotlight is always going to fall on them. It's not. Sometimes the spotlight ignores them completely. Think of the places you have shied away from because, in your words, "Everybody will notice me." Consider the teenager who is convinced that, in spite of hours and dollars spent in preparation, he or she is unfit to be noticed. Said teen is convinced that his/her jeans are too loose … too tight … too old … too new … too long … too short …to bogue … too nerdy … or have the wrong label stitched on the rump. Or if the jeans are all right, then it's the zits, the spots, the split ends or the retainer that "everybody will notice," And no words to the contrary can convince them that they are no more nerd-like than anybody else. And, even if they are, most other teenagers are too inwardly focused on their own imperfections to notice anybody elses.

But I know how they feel. It's the same thing that makes me feel uncomfortable on the dance floor. I am certain that everybody else in the room is a second cousin to Arthur Murray and will immediately cease and desist everything else they are doing in order to watch me dance. (Actually, that sometimes happens, given the fact that there are still a great many people who don't expect to see a dancing preacher. "Look, Maude, the man dances." "Yes, Marvin, but so badly.") People like me, the teens, and the rest of the center stage phobics need to hear an occasional word that says, "Relax! The universe doesn't even know you exist!"

Similarly in need of that advice are the "Messiah complex" folks among us. These are the people who believe that they have been singularly called to do it all, carry it all, solve everything and save everyone. I think of the young man who had just received an apprentice plumber's certificate and celebrated by taking his wife to Niagara Falls. Squinting into the sun while watching the roaring water cascade over the precipice, he announced (with deep solemnity), "Honey, I think I can fix this."

I understand that, too. Because for a whole lot of reasons that are too personal and complex to go into here. I tend to see myself as a fixer, and have sometimes felt burdened by the same sense of obligation that feeling has introduced into my life. Somebody needs to question both my competence and my motivation. Somebody needs to occasionally look me in the eye and say, "Ritter, you can't fix every leak. What's more, you don't need to. Believing that you can, and must, not only says that you are more than a little self-deluded, it also says that you don't really trust God. He is the court of last resort, not you."

John Baille reports that during the blitz bombing of London during World War II, a woman explained how she was able to sleep nights by saying, "I finally figured out that since God slumbers not nor sleeps, there was no good reason both of us should stay awake." That's good theology. I try to remember it at three o'clock in the morning when the budget beats back the blessings of sleep. At such moments it is good to remind myself of my insignificance. It also helps me to focus on the fact that the only way to bear burdens is to share them.

Ah! Enough of that. Let's reach into the other pocket. The paper, please. Here it is. "**For you, Ritter, the entire universe was created.**" Wow! All this? For me? You've got to be kidding. Please say you are not kidding. For I need to hear this. I have a lot of friends who need to hear this. There are times in which I need the lifting word … the age-defying word … the word that causes me to soar.

I am convinced that one of the reasons the verse poem "Desiderata" became so popular was the chorus that began: "You are a child of the universe; no less than the trees and stars, you have a right to be here." And to people who have a hard time taking themselves seriously (or significantly), and who number themselves among the folded, spindled and mutilated victims of society, such news is good news indeed.

The psalmist rendered the same opinion. We heard it a few moments ago. What is man that God is mindful of him? Well, man is something special indeed. Barely less than God. Brightest among the stars. Crowned over all. Commissioned to greatness. Lord of all things, made and unmade. To man, God says, "Let your significance consist in the fact that I have given you the responsibility of looking after my stuff. And let it also consist in the fact that I have invited you to bask in my glory."

This is the theme echoed throughout the Old Testament and driven home in the New, causing the Danish philosopher, Soren Kirkegaard to write, "When I read the New Testament, I get the impression that everyone is supposed to be a giant." And so we are. Meant to be giants, that is.

But the real clue to our significance does not come from our place in the pecking order of creation (somewhere above mosquitoes, swamp rats, white rhinos, draft horses, and great simian apes). Neither does it come from any particular task we have been assigned (such as populating the earth, naming the animals, having dominion over the birds and the fish, or taking out the garbage). No, the clue to our significance is contained in the fact that God knows us, cares about us, and (in some strange way) is diminished when we are not relating to Him, or are rejecting His overtures.

Of all the miracles in the Bible, the most amazing one is that God should, or could, be interested in me. Reconsider the eighth Psalm. We read, " What is man that thou are mindful of him?" But isn't it amazing that God should be "mindful" of us at all … that we are "in" His mind, or "on" His mind, in the first place? Willie Nelson wasn't the first to sing, "You were always on my mind."

William Sloane Coffin, around whose ministry swirls controversy like dust balls around a moving broom, never spoke more softly and tenderly than when he wrote: "I am daily impressed that we are but a tiny dot on the edge of a star cluster, in a universe that has millions of star clusters just like it. But that leads me to dwell less on my unimportance than to marvel at a God who cares for me as if He or She had nothing else to care for." This was the same sentiment with which Mahalia Jackson brought down the house, night after night, when she would close her eyes and sing, "His eye is on the sparrow, and I know He watches me."

That notion defies comprehension. How does God do it? After all, He's got so many. Well, I'm not sure how God does it. The mechanics of such "watchfulness" totally escape me. But if I trust that promise, what a marvelous effect it produces in my life.

Recall, if you can, a time when you learned that your presence in someone else's universe was not as anonymous or unappreciated as you had previously thought. Perhaps it was the day that you were summoned to the office of someone in management, known previously to you only by reputation. Once there, you were welcomed, promoted, given a raise, and invested with an opportunity that even you were not sure you were ready to assume. And in answer to your half-stammered exclamation of surprise, you were told: "Some of us have had our eye on you for a long time."

Or perhaps you were very much in need and some casual acquaintance (little more than a stranger, really) discerned your need, addressed it, and left you with the feeling that there was nothing else that he or she needed to be doing, at that moment, that was more important than "being there" for you.

Or perhaps it was a chance meeting with a certain special "someone," that you later discovered was not nearly as "chance" as you thought. Although you had never laid eyes on her in your life, she had seen something in you, and positioned herself so as to be in the path of your turning … when you turned … quite "accidentally," of course.

How good it feels to know that we are known. How good it feels to see that we are seen. And where the lonely, longing eyes of God are at work, none of us (no matter how insignificant or obscure) is ever lost in the shuffle.

We noted, earlier, the biblical conviction that God slumbers not nor sleeps. Is God an insomniac? No! It's just that He, like many of us, finds it hard to close His eyes and nod off until every last one of the kids is home.

September 10, 1989
Nardin Park United Methodist Church
Farmington Hills, Michigan

Note: The ancient parable, "A Tale of Two Pockets," first appeared in a sermon by the late Dr. Duncan Littlefair of Fountain Street Church, Grand Rapids, Michigan, nearly fifty years ago.

The Rev. Dr. William Sloane Coffin's words appeared in a sermon reprint from Riverside Church in New York City.

The Rev. Dr. Barry Johnson was the source of both his own quote earlier in this sermon and the fable by Anthony deMello, a Jesuit priest and psychotherapist from India. At the time Barry first shared this material, he was the preaching minister at First Community Church in Columbus, Ohio.

3

THERE ARE BEARS IN THE WILDERNESS

My friend, Dr. Carl Price, joined forces with me in Birmingham after an illustrious 25-year run at Midland UMC. During our years together, Carl regularly took a group of church members on two-week hiking trips (ranging from Alaska to Maine). As one more comfortable with cities, I love the stories these people told upon returning from the mountains. I have had little experience (read that as "none") hiking in the wilderness. But, in a broader sense, I have lived in the wilderness during many periods of my life. As have you, dear reader. As have you.

Scripture: Genesis 32:22-32

Let's start with a short list. The third dumbest thing I ever did in my life was to park my car on the rim of an Upper Peninsula dump near the town of Paradise on a Monday night in 1968 so that I could watch scrawny bears come out at dusk, paw through the mountain of trash bags and forage for garbage. The second dumbest thing I ever did in my life was to go back to the same rim, of the same dump, to watch the same bears paw through the same garbage on Tuesday night in Paradise. And the first dumbest thing I ever did was to go through the same drill, with the same bears, on Wednesday night in Paradise. Which only proves that Paradise isn't. Or that "yours truly" is easily entertained. Although I was far from alone on that rim, given that my then-very-young wife was beside me, and 20 or 30 cars (which, by Wednesday, had become quite familiar) were parked around me. For, once the sun slid over the yardarm in Paradise, the bears and the garbage were the only game in town.

Truth be told, I know next to nothing about bears. I hear that there are some in Chicago … little ones at Wrigley Field … monster ones at Soldier Field. And I know that bears tend to group themselves under common family names like Brown, Black, Polar, Kodiak, and Grizzly. I hear that some are more dangerous than others … although we non-north-woodsy types had all fear domesticated out of us as children by the likes of Teddy Bear, Yogi Bear, Paddington Bear, and (especially) Pooh Bear, whose adventures with everything from honey pots to heffalumps brought me great pleasure once and, whenever I stumble upon them today, bring me great pleasure still. And while you are pondering your own youthful association with bears, I would have you consider this. It comes from an author named Lawrence Kushner, lifted from a book entitled Invisible Line of Connection …

The first time my wife Karen and I were up in the mountains of Montana, we were awed and even a little frightened by the scale and power of the wilderness.

Whether buildings or bridges or even hiking trails, the creations of human beings seemed by comparison precariously inadequate, hopelessly finite, fragile. Back East, nature must be preserved and revered. High in the Rockies, it was the opposite. Here, we had to be wary of nature lest, in a blind moment, she consume us all. Everywhere, signs warned of bears. They can run, swim, and climb faster than any human being. And they have been known to attack without provocation. Stories circulate about an unwary hiker, just a few months ago, who ...

Karen and I drove up to the end of the road at Two Medicine Lake, where there is a log cabin, general store, and a little boat that can ferry you to the trailhead on the far shore. Inside, watching hummingbirds dart to and fro around a feeder, having a cup of coffee, I met Charlie Slocum, a retired biology teacher from Minnesota, who spends his summers working for the National Park Service. In the pristine Eden air, I understood why he had returned for a score of summers. But I was also more than casually concerned about being eaten by a grizzly.

"Get many bears up here, do you?" I asked.

"Sometimes we get quite a few."

"How about on that easy trail around the lake over there? Any chance of running into any this morning – so near the store?"

He paused long enough to hear the question behind the question and took a slow sip of his coffee. " If I could tell you for sure there wouldn't be any bears, it wouldn't be the wilderness, now, would it?"

I thanked him for his candor, and we went on our hike. Maybe that is all it ever comes down to: You can walk where things are predictable … or you can enter the wilderness. Without the wilderness, there can be neither reverence nor revelation.

All things considered, it is Carl Price who should be preaching this sermon. I am the city boy. Carl is the country boy. It is Carl who knows trails. And it is Carl who knows Grizzlies. And if you are numbered among the seventy who will be hiking in Glacier National Park later this summer with Carl, this is not a sermon meant to deter you. Yes, there are bears there. But Carl will tell you how to avoid 'em and outsmart 'em … everything but out-run 'em (which Carl knew was impossible, even when he had good knees).

But both Carl and I know that there is more to the wilderness than Montana. And both Carl and I know that bears come in multiple sizes and disguises, to the degree that meeting one is nigh unto unavoidable.

Let's start with the wilderness. It's everywhere. One finds it in every region and in every religion. I know of no religion without one or more wilderness stories. They are universal. People wander in the wilderness. Others, including Jesus, are tried,

A photograph taken by Carl Price while leading one of the trail hikes for which he was famous.

tested, even tempted in the wilderness. Still others are banished to the wilderness ... or (having entered it) are given up for lost in the wilderness.

Fairy tales, too, are full of wilderness. In fairy tales, the wilderness is sometimes called "the woods" ... other times, "the forest." Such places are enchanted for some, "foreboding" for others. It depends on how you arrive there the first time you go there. Do you approach the wilderness merrily or warily? Does your fairy godmother guide you through it, or does your wicked stepmother abandon you in it?

I find it interesting ... although not surprising ... that Larry and Karen Kushner were not deterred from their hike by anything Charlie Slocum told them about Grizzlies. As they wrote: "Maybe that is all it ever comes down to. You can walk where it is predictable. Or you can enter the wilderness. But

41

Reverend Dr. Carl Price is an esteemed United Methodist pastor, a most accomplished preacher, and a dear friend. Carl joined our staff at Birmingham First UMC following his retirement at First UMC in Midland, Michigan.

without the wilderness, there can be neither reverence nor revelation. "

Which is an interesting suggestion. For, Kushner is suggesting that there are "good things" to be gained by going where the bears go. Certainly, there are Indian tribes who equate a fortnight in the wilderness with a young man's ticket price to adulthood. He goes into the wilderness as a boy. He comes out of the wilderness a man.

Today, girls make similar journeys. This nation (anyway) does not lack for Outward Bound type programs. There are many who believe that all of us could benefit from them, even as severely troubled teenagers often find their best-last-chance of salvation wrapped up in them. To be sure, there are risks attendant to such ventures (as kids from Cranbrook Upper School discovered a few years back). But I don't see any lessening of their appeal. Which means that there must be benefits there … even blessings. Did I say, "blessings?" Well, yes, I did. But for the moment, hold the thought, trusting that I'll eventually circle back to it.

If I have any quarrel with Larry Kushner, it's with his notion that you can choose to walk where things are predictable. You can't. That's because the wilderness is a creeping thing, which has its way of finding you. Meaning that you can meet a bear almost anywhere.

Which brings me to a lady named Nurya Love Parish who met one in church … and she's a preacher. I don't know where she preaches regularly. But on a number of occasions, she has filled the pulpit of a large independent congregation in Grand Rapids, which has spent three of its last four years without a senior minister.

The first time she preached there, she met a man who subsequently became her husband. That meeting took place in the hand-shaking, coffee-sipping, small-talking moments after the service. The second time she preached there, the queasiness she felt in her middle parts (she later learned) had less to do with anxiety than pregnancy. And following the third time she preached there, she learned that her husband's 104 degree fever was not, as she thought, a precursor of the flu, so much as an announcement of lymphoma.

Three visits. Three sermons. Three surprises. Two good ones. One not so good one. Funny that she should equate church with wilderness. Funnier still that she should equate cancer with a bear. Which it is, of course. A real bear, I mean. Not the woodsy one. But a formidable one. Which only goes to prove that if you go walking long enough, you'll meet a bear or two … maybe even four or more. So how, pray tell, will you live in their presence?

Hold that thought, too, for a minute. Let's jump to Jacob. Jacob of Genesis fame. Son of Isaac. Father of Joseph. Brother of Esau … whom, as you will remember, Jacob screwed over royally. And pretty much got away with it. Sure, he had to vacate the country for a few years. But like the cream in the milk bottle I drank from as a child, Jacob floated back to the top. He had a beautiful wife. Multiple kids. Lots of servants. Plenty of money.

Now, twenty years later, Jacob is coming home. His plan is to make peace with Esau. The final night of his journey, he camps (alone) along the river. Where something … someone … shows up and tackles him. Clean out of the blue. The fight goes on all night. First, the stranger winning … then Jacob winning … then the stranger winning. But as daybreak threatens to illuminate the arena, the stranger realizes that the tide is turning (slowly, but inevitably) back toward Jacob. So the stranger gives Jacob a low blow, throwing Jacob's hip out of joint (permanently). Then the stranger … the nocturnal adversary … makes like he's going to leave.

Which is where the story gets a little bit weird. For, if I were Jacob, "leaving" is exactly what I'd want the stranger to do. "Yes, by all means, go. Get out of here. Sooner rather than later. You've ambushed me. You've battled me. Now you've crippled me. Be gone."

Amazingly, Jacob doesn't say that. Instead, while holding his adversary in a vice-like grip, he says, "I will not let you go unless you bless me."

So, who is Jacob fighting … in the wilderness … at night … all night … through the night?

God?
   Maybe.

An angel of God?
   Maybe.

His own guilt?
   Maybe.

All three?
   Maybe.

We're never gonna know. And it matters relatively little if we ever know. All we need to know is that Jacob's foe is an adversary with the power to cripple. And if you have never met one of those in your life so far … an adversary with the power to cripple, I mean … you are darned lucky. Because there are bears in the wilderness. And because the wilderness creeps, so as to become unavoidable.

Well, what about the blessing, you ask. I told you I'd return to it. Notice, dear friends, that (in this beloved Bible story) the blessing does not precede the attack ("Hi ho, hi ho, how blessedly I go."). Nor does the blessing prevent the attack. No, the blessing is sought (and received) in the attack … from the attacker. It is as if Jacob is saying:

> Can I … even from this … even in the midst of this … this, which I did not want, did not seek, and did everything I could possibly do to avoid … can I experience something … receive something … learn something … that will deepen my reverence for life and reveal something of God that I had not seen before, and would have most likely missed, had this not happened?

It's not totally unlike the little boy who, when confronted with a roomful of manure on Christmas morning, choked back his tears and began searching for the pony that he knew had to be in there somewhere.

I don't pretend that this is easy. For, like you, I am not in the habit of seeking blessings after all-night fights. And, if the Jacob story is correct, such blessings don't necessarily pop out at you (or feel like manna from heaven dropping on top of you).

Sometimes you have to hold on for dear life and scream: "Give me something ... show me something ... that I can get in no other way."

Go back to cancer, which hits many in the night. For even if you receive the diagnosis at high noon, the word (itself) tends to turn everything dark.

Sometimes I compare cancer to a stranger with a suitcase who walks up your steps ... strolls across your porch ... and rings your doorbell. But when you open the door, he says nary a word. Instead, he walks past you and starts climbing the stairs to your second story. Following him, you protest ... wanting to know who he is ... wondering what he thinks he is doing. Tersely, he answers that he is moving into your front bedroom. You tell him that your front bedroom is not available for occupancy. You tell him that you have not advertised bedrooms for boarders. You tell him that you are not looking for someone to move in ... don't want someone to move in ... and have neither time nor space for someone to move in. You even tell him you can't understand how someone would just ignore your wishes and barge in anyway. But, all this aside, the stranger is unpacking his suitcase ... moving your stuff ... making room for his stuff ... socks and underwear in the dresser drawers ... slacks and shirts in the closet.

Unable, at least at that moment, to evict him, you have to decide two things:

How are you going to live with your
front room occupied?

Is there anything that this experience
can add to your life?

Some people wrestle with those questions. Other people run from those questions. The difference between the wrestlers and the runners is the difference between those who are living with cancer and those who are dying from cancer.

After hearing this sermon, I figure 70 of you will pick up the phone tomorrow morning and call Carl Price ... if, for no other reason than to ask:

> "Carl, pardon my bothering you in the middle of a busy summer. But, as concerns this place you are taking us, are there (perchance) any bears there?"

Which is an acceptable question, deserving an honest answer. But let it be followed by a second question. One that goes something like this:

> "Carl, as concerns this place you are taking us
> this summer, is there (perchance) any beauty there?"

Bears?   Beauty?
Bears?   Beauty?
Bears?   Beauty?

Funny isn't it, that life doesn't offer "beauty or the beast." No, the second word in that popular phrase is not "or." The second word is "and."

June 30, 2002
First United Methodist Church
Birmingham, Michigan

*A group of wilderness hikers from First United Methodist Church
in Birmingham led by Carl Price.*

*Note: Obviously, I owe a debt of gratitude to both Lawrence
Kushner and Nurya Love Parish for their contributions to this
sermon. Lawrence Kushner's book, Invisible Line of Connection,
was excerpted by the Christian Century in June of 2002. Nurya
Love Parish was serving as an interim minister at Fountain Street
Church in Grand Rapids, Michigan where her remarks became
available in a sermon reprint early in the year 2002.*

4

SHOULD I LIVE TO BE A HUNDRED

As I was proofreading these chapters, a very dear colleague called to tell me he is dying. In a very warm and personal way, he asked me if, when the time came, I would fly to Texas to preach his funeral. He also told me he was" ready to go." The trouble is, I don't know if I'm ready to "have him go." Or "go" myself for that matter. I talked about this (in the pulpit) as far back as 1997. But I suppose it will always be a work in progress.

Scripture: Jeremiah 20 (selected verses)

There was a story that first appeared in a newspaper in Galveston, Texas about a woman and her parakeet named "Chippie." It seems that the woman was cleaning Chippie's cage with a canister vacuum cleaner, the kind that has one of those long suction tubes onto which you put the various attachments. On this particular occasion, she was cleaning the bottom of the cage with no attachments on the tube, when the phone rang.

You guessed it. At the precise moment she was saying, "hello" into the mouthpiece, she was listening to the horrible sound of something being sucked into the vacuum. That something was Chippie.

She immediately put down the phone, ripped open the vacuum bag, and found Chippie inside, stunned but still alive. Since the bird was covered with dust and soot, she grabbed it, ran into the bathroom, turned on the faucet, and held the bird under a full stream of water in order to clean it off. When she finished, she spotted her hair dryer on the bathroom sink. Turning it on, she held Chippie in front of the blast of hot air, the better to dry him off.

Somehow that story began to make the rounds until it finally caught an editor's ear at the local newspaper office. It must have been a very slow news day in Galveston because they sent a reporter to do a follow-up. After confirming all of the aforementioned details, the reporter concluded the interview by asking, "How's Chippie doing now?" "Well," she said, "Chippie doesn't seem physically any the worse for wear. But he doesn't sing much anymore. He just sort of sits there and stares." And who could blame him? I know the feeling. So do you. We've all experienced something like that. Life treats us kinda rough, ruffling our feathers a bit, to the point where we don't feel much like singing either.

And when the song goes, so does our confidence. We never sit quite so easy in the saddle again. For, if we have been thrown once, we can be thrown again. It leads us to view the future with what Cameron Murchison calls "a pervasive agnosticism."

Chippie knows the feeling, which is why he stares rather than sings.

And some never get past that; the "roughing up" they experience leads to anger and bitterness. "Life is cruel." "Life is unfair." "I didn't ask for this." "I don't deserve this." The Danish philosopher, Soren Kierkegaard, once described a man who lived his life as if he were a typographical error. "Look at me," he cried to the world at large. "Look at God's great mistake. I am living proof that God neither catches nor rectifies every error ... every omission ... every wrong."

That anger can also lead to despair. Moments ago, I served you a slice of one of the great Hebrew prophets. His name was Jeremiah. And before his life was history, he both said and did some amazing things. But Jeremiah also had a tendency to get horribly down on himself ... on everyone else ... on life in general ... and on God in particular. Listen, again, to Chapter 20.

> A curse on the day I was born,
> On the day my mother bore me,
> On the man who brought my father the news.
> Why did that man not kill me in the womb,
> So that the womb would have been my tomb?
> Why did I ever come out to live in toil and sorrow,
> And to end my days in shame?

That's more than just "a pervasive agnosticism about the future." That's a pervasive regret about the past. The Jeremiah who spoke those words did not just sit and stare. He lamented.

To be sure, not everyone turns to anger and despair. Some turn to fatalism. Wendell Berry tells the story of the baptism of King Aengus by none other than St. Patrick (sometime in the middle of the fifth century). During the baptism, St. Patrick leaned on his sharp-pointed staff and inadvertently stabbed the king's foot. After the baptism was over, Patrick looked down at all the blood. Realizing what he had done, he begged the king's forgiveness. "Why did you suffer in silence?" said Patrick to his king. The king replied, "I thought it was a part of the ritual."

And many people still think that way. They think that pain is part of the ritual ... that the inadvertent stabbings of life go with the territory ... and that there is no use saying anything to the priests because they are merely the dealers of a hand that God has already stacked against them.

Norman Cousins talks about being sent to a tuberculosis sanitarium at the age of ten. Terribly frail and underweight, he quickly discerned that his fellow patients divided themselves into two groups. One group consisted of those who were confident they would beat the disease, while those in the other group resigned themselves to a prolonged and even fatal illness. Cousins noted that the optimistic ones quickly became good friends and had little to do with the others who resigned themselves to the worst. Then he adds, "When newcomers arrived on the floor, we did our best to recruit them before the bleak brigade could go to work."

And make no mistake about it, the "bleak brigade" is out there ... for us, even as it was for him. But listen to what Cousins says next:

> Even at the age of ten, I became aware that the boys in my group had a far higher percentage of "discharged as cured" outcomes than the kids in the other group. And the lessons I learned about "hope" in that sanitarium played an important role in my recovery then ... and in my feelings since ... about the preciousness of life.

Don't miss the irony in that. For in the aftermath of being roughed up by illness ... in a sanitarium where it is probably easier to stare than sing ... and while fending off the boys of the "bleak brigade" ... Cousins came to the realization that life was incredibly precious and ought always be enjoyed for the gift that it is.

As many of you know, Bruce Hayden is a fan of Bernie Siegel and has taught a course on Siegel's book *Love, Medicine and Miracles.* What you probably do not know is the degree to which Siegel has built on Norman Cousins' work, especially as concerns his involvement with a group that he calls "Exceptional Cancer Patients." They are deemed exceptional, not because of their medical prognosis but because of the quality of self that they bring to the fight. Writes Siegel:

> To find out whether you have the outlook of an exceptional patient, ask yourself a simple question. Do you want to live to be a hundred? In our Exceptional Patients Group, we have found the answer to be an immediate and visceral "Yes."

He goes on to say that most of us will answer that question with a qualified "Yes," but seldom with a visceral one. We will say: "Of course I'd like to be a hundred …

> … if you can guarantee I'll be healthy."
> … if you can guarantee I won't be alone."
> … if you can guarantee I won't outlive my savings."

I can understand that. If someone were to ask me about the attractiveness of celebrating my one-hundredth birthday, I'd attach all of those qualifications and probably add one or two more. "Exceptional patients," however, know that life comes with no guarantees. Yet they are willing to accept the risks as well as the challenges. They do not fear external events. They know that happiness is an inside job.

Obviously, there is nothing magical about reaching the century mark. Obviously, nobody wants to hang on, merely for the sake of hanging on. Obviously, most of us will reach a point where life's "preciousness" has been so compromised by the loss of mind or function, that letting go will seem like an act of faith rather than an act of surrender. But when "exceptional patients" let go, it is not out of fear, so much as fatigue. Exceptional people go out, not as frightened lambs, but as tired lions.

The people who want to reach one hundred are not blind to life's circumstances. Neither are they unrealistic about life's pitfalls. They have simply chosen to take life as it comes, without holding out for better terms. What does that mean? It means they know that life, itself, is the gift … not the better terms.

Many of you know Rick Lange. For a number of years, Rick served as the scoutmaster of our church-sponsored Boy Scout troop. And last week, Rick's wife, Barb, was in charge of feeding us so magnificently. But I doubt that any of you know Rick's great-aunt, Helen Ewbanks. Helen is the matriarch of one of the proud old families of Albion. She still lives in her home near the campus, although she summers at Bayview, the United Methodist enclave on Little Traverse Bay near Petoskey, Michigan. At 93, she is slowing down some but is still an amazing lady. Which I can echo in spades.

When I was lecturing at Bayview, she listened to me every day. You can literally see the gears move in Helen's mind, so keen and exciting is her intellect. She knows she has had a good ride. And she knows it won't last forever. As the hymn suggests, "Time like an ever-rolling stream bears all its sons away" … and then doubles back for its daughters. On the day my lectures were complete, she said, "I hope they get you back here … soon." Then, knowing she had exposed the issue of her own mortality, she added (with sparkling eyes), "I've lived long enough to see the comet at the beginning of the century and, again, at century's end. The next time it returns, I won't be around to see it. But look up. I'll be the one riding its tail."

People like Helen are walking acts of praise. Because they live it, they don't necessarily have to sing it or say it. But most of them do anyway because their enjoyment spontaneously overflows in thanks and praise.

Well, you say, that comes easy when life always smiles on you. Helen Ewbanks, for example, will be the first to admit that she needs a computer to count her many blessings. But I would couple her testimony with that of another Helen, who can count her blessings on a hand and a half. That's because her hands are severely crippled (along with the rest of her body). But in surveying the acreage of her life from the sclerotic wreckage of her twisted frame, she was once heard to say, "I wouldn't have missed 'being' for anything."

If only these two old Helens could teach the young … especially those (among the young) who reach the point where they can no longer see life's beauty through its burden.

Two weeks ago, we gathered on a Monday afternoon … 700 strong … shoehorning ourselves into every nook and cranny of this sanctuary. We came to say good-bye to, and offer prayers for, Maggie Roberts … done (at age 21) much too soon … and dead (of her own hand) much too tragically. As you know, the landscape of such a service is hard for me, but certainly not strange to me, having walked it (as the old song says) from both sides now.

In preparing my sermon, I talked with Matt and Jane and Doug, along with Maggie's sisters, Darrah and Charlotte. During the course of those conversations, they told me many things. But one thing they told me was not to skirt the cause of Maggie's death or sugarcoat the pain of Maggie's choice. They told me that there would be a lot of young people at Maggie's service … some of them, confused … some of them, troubled … and a few of them, every bit as fragile as Maggie had been.

Then they said, "Don't let any of those kids walk away thinking that Maggie's death was good, or that Maggie's choice was (in any conceivable way) glamorous."

So I looked at those kids and said something like this: "While we can derive some comfort from the fact that Maggie is now free (and she had a lot to be free from), as a freedom movement, hers was more tragic than heroic … certainly, not the kind that gives rise to folk songs in the cabaret or parades in the street. While her choice of death is certainly understandable, it is far from applaudable." My friends, whatever the circumstances of our living, we are not supposed to look a gift life in the mouth.

Annie Dillard writes: "I would like to imagine that the dying pray, at the last, not 'please' but 'thank you' … simply for the privilege of having been invited to the party."

In one sense, I understand that image. For Kris and I often leave Saturday night wedding receptions early so that I can appear bright-eyed and moderately-intelligent by 8:15 on Sunday mornings. And just before leaving, we cruise the hall (dodging the dancers), seeking out our host and hostess to thank them for the privilege of being there.

But while that image speaks to me, I find one small part of it uncomfortable. My problem is not with thanking the host. My problem is with leaving the party early. So, if it is all right with you, I'll thank the Host now … later … today … tomorrow … daily … continually … whatever. But if it's all right with the Host, I'll prefer to stick around.

November 23, 1997
First United Methodist Church
Birmingham, Michigan

Note: For more on the work of both Norman Cousins and Bernie Siegel, see Siegel's book, Love, Medicine and Miracles, published by MSFO Books in 1984. Annie Dillard's of-quoted line about being invited to the party can be found in her book, The Writing Life published by Harper Perennial in 1989.

Maggie Roberts on a Lake Michigan beach ...
where she found solace.

5

PRELIMINARY NOTES ON A LIVING WILL TO BE SHARED WITH MY DAUGHTER

Kris and I have had wills for as long as I can remember. Ours were most recently updated a little more than a year ago. We also have medical directives, so that someone will know, at some crucial moment, what our wishes are. But fear not. What follows will read like a sermon, not a legal document. After all, theology (not law, medicine, or even economics) is the only profession in which I am moderately proficient.

Scripture: 2 Corinthians 4:16 - 5:8

Just the other day, I received the gift of a wonderful new book, personally autographed by its author. Entitled *The Undertaking: Life Studies from the Dismal Trade*, it consists of some well-seasoned reflections by Tom Lynch, who, with his family, has been in the funeral business longer than many of us have been alive. He begins:

Every year I bury a couple hundred of my townspeople. Another two or three dozen I take to the crematory to be burned. I sell caskets, burial vaults, and urns for the ashes, along with a sideline in headstones and monuments. I do flowers on commission.

Apart from the tangibles, I sell the use of my building: 11,000 square feet, furnished and fixtures, with an abundance of pastels, chair rails, and crown moldings. The whole lash-up is mortgaged and remortgaged, well into the next century. My rolling stock includes a hearse, two Fleetwoods, and a minivan with darkened windows (which our price list calls a "service vehicle" and which everyone else in town call the "dead wagon").

Tom did not select his profession, so much as he was born into it. He recalls pondering the meaning of his father's trade and the unique childhood problem of having to respond to the inquiries of his friends asking what his daddy did.

> He's an undertaker, I would say. He takes people under. Get it? Underground. Which would usually shut them up. Still, I was never as certain as I tried to sound. I wondered why my father wasn't an "underputter" … you know, the one who "puts" people underground. "Taking them" seemed a bit excessive. I mean, if they were dead, they wouldn't need company on the way. Would they?

I suppose there is certain morbidity to all of this, or else Tom Lynch wouldn't refer to it as "the dismal trade." But if so, it is morbidity rooted in inevitability ... what with death being more certain than even taxes. For some can dodge taxes. But even the most nimble-footed can't dodge death. My friend, Emery Percell (who preaches in Rockford, Illinois), startled me this summer when he reminded me that everybody Jesus ever healed, died. Even Lazarus, whom Jesus raised from the tomb, returned to it ... sooner or later. Which is a thought that can make you depressed ... or philosophical. But it can also make you appreciative ... for what is. Which is where Ralph Finch comes out (assuming you have read the piece that graces the cover of Steeple Notes this morning). Having outlived every male in his family at the still-tender age of 57, he concludes:

> As to who lives, how long, and why, I will leave those ponderous questions to greater minds. I am here, and I don't know why. Why me? Why them? I'll keep my sanity, thank you, and not attempt to reason it out. I'll simply thank God for having had the luck of the draw 57 times. Maybe this year ...

> Still, the subject here is really life, not death. Once you accept and acknowledge death, you begin to appreciate life all the more. And I am greedy enough to want more.

I appreciate Ralph's words, given that I have lived Ralph's years. To the exact number. We are the same age. And, following in Ralph's stead, this is the year that I will outlive my father. What's been has been good. But I'd like a whole lot more. Having spent an inordinate amount of the last three months burying people (along with bidding farewell to a princess and a saint ... Diana and Teresa), I find that it is not death that is rubbing off on me, but life. As death becomes more real, I find that I would just as soon forestall it. Not avoid it. Not deny it. Not repress it. Just forestall it. I want to live.

But I am also growing older. In the initial draft of this morning's sermon, I wrote the line, "Most days I don't think about getting older." Then I crossed it out because it isn't true. Most days I do think about it.

Just this week they wrote me a letter from the Albion Alumni Office. "This is your 35th reunion," they told me. "Come see your friends." Which I probably won't do, given that I need to put in an appearance at Vision 2000 in the morning, and marry a couple of nice kids in the afternoon. I trust my "friends" will understand. Ten years ago, I did attend my 25th reunion. I also answered a request for a one-page letter for inclusion in a book to be shared with the members of my anniversary class. The letter was supposed to describe the most important things that have happened in my first quarter of a century after graduation.

I wrote it. But it wasn't easy. In the last sentence of my first paragraph, I said: "It comes as a bit of a surprise to realize how uninspiring my life has been." Which I can't say anymore. And in the last sentence of the last paragraph I wrote: "All in all, life has not been without a certain sweetness." While today I might be more inclined to quote Flannery O'Connor who suffered terribly from Lupus for years. Just before she died at age 39, she wrote to a friend, "I can, with one eye squinted, take it all as a blessing." Which is why I am quite willing to go for more … life that is. I am willing to chance additional surprises, given that I hunger after additional sweetness. What is hard to admit is that 35 years have now been tucked under my belt since I last saw the people with whom I graduated. The thought weighs heavy on me … along with a lot of other stuff that I carry under my belt.

But, it has also occurred to me that I should give some thought to future things, that I might better enjoy present things. There isn't a week goes by that someone doesn't call me up, send me a letter, or invite me to a seminar so that I might give serious thought to planning my later years. What they mean is "economic planning," of which I have done a fair amount. If I die tomorrow, you will not have to throw a benefit for me. And if I die tomorrow, nobody will suffer financially. Which also means that if I live tomorrow, I will probably have more than enough to see me through to the grave. So much for economics.

But what about other things? How else might I prepare? I find myself captivated by those beautiful lines of Paul, written to the Corinthians, " So we do not lose heart. Though our outer nature be wasting away, our inner nature is being renewed, day by day." I find myself waiting for that to happen. I find myself wanting to discover exactly how that happens. For I know that I have less and less control over my "outer nature" that is wasting away. But there is still a lot I can do about my "inner nature," and the possibility of its day-to-day renewal. For if I can get my "inner nature" in better shape, I may even be able to slow down the degree to which my "outer nature" wastes away.

I have been around enough "vintage Christians" (how's that as a synonym for "elderly") to know that what's "inside" has as much to do with the process of aging as what's "outside." It is never too early to work on one's "inner nature." The aging process only exaggerates the personality of our younger years, both as to our graces and our idiosyncrasies. In other words, the gracious ones become even more gracious. And the cranky ones … you figure it out. Not so long ago, a few of us were quietly discussing a lady who, in her dotage, complains about everything and everyone. Someone, overhearing our conversation, had known the lady for a great many years. Her comment was instructive. "Nothing's changed," was all she said. "Nothing's changed."

Therefore, there are some "inner nature" things that I want to work on now, so that they might serve me later. For one thing, I want to work on my emotional independence. Don't get me wrong. I do not mean emotional distance or emotional withdrawal. I mean freedom from emotional dependencies. I want to love and be loved, without feeling that loving me is somebody's obligation. I want to work on the issue of my own happiness, without falling into the trap of thinking it is somebody's job to make me happy. It isn't anybody's job to make me happy. It isn't my wife's job. It isn't my daughter's job. It isn't my bishop's job. It's my job. And while I'm doing my job, I want to grow increasingly comfortable with my own company. Because if I do not like being with myself, how will I ever face the prospect of being alone?

But, even as I work on emotional independence, I want to cultivate more genuine friendships. Much of my life has been oriented toward tasks and goals. But it has not gone unnoticed by me that the older people I admire most, often have friendships stretching over 50 years. Is it possible that I could learn to live with fewer victories if I had more companions? Which leads to the realization that, at this point in my life, the growing edge of marriage is friendship. Somewhere along that marital journey, I realized that my wife is my best friend. And has probably always been my best friend.

I have also set for myself the goal of forming an adult relationship with you, dear daughter. To be sure, I am very much your father. I will always be your father. I doubt that I will ever lose the title (or the responsibilities) that go with being your father. But if I am never anything but your father, you will never be anything but my daughter. And when children become adults, they do not spend much time in the company of people who continually make them feel like children.

Moreover, I want to keep working on something important. I have a lot of friends who are talking about early retirements. For the life of me, I can't fathom waking up tomorrow and not being able to go to work, doing what I do now. But that day will come. Someday, I hope to retire about six months before somebody asks me why I didn't. But, even then, I hope to keep going and growing. I realize that I will be less afraid of dying, to the degree that I minimize any regrets I may have about living. So far, I am doing all right on that score. If I "checked out" tomorrow, I might mourn the unfinished canvas of my life. But I'd be willing to let the picture stand as it is.

Yet, I keep working on that picture. Time doesn't stand still. Neither should I. Which means that I must learn to walk the line between making peace with my imperfections (and the imperfections of the world) without becoming completely resigned to them. Berthold Brecht says it well when he writes:

There are people who struggle for a day, and they are good. There are others who struggle for many years, and they are good. And there are those who struggle all their lives. They are the indispensable ones.

In that vein, I have discovered a rather strange correlation in life. Every time I get overly comfortable with things I become mildly depressed.

These are some of the "inner nature" things I need to work on. Having shared them, let me shift gears so that I might speak about the very late years of my life. I call them the "very late years," because I don't have the faintest idea when I shall live them. Their "lateness" will have more to do with the date of my death, than with the number of my birthdays. Or, as I once said, the "late years" are those in which the shadow comes earlier and earlier in the day, blocking out more and more of the light. How do I wish to live the late years? What follows is both personal and preliminary. It does not need to fit you. In time, it may not fit me. Everybody needs a little space in the margin for a rewrite.

First, as concerns location, it is my hope that I never become so wedded to real estate that I conclude my life is over if, and when, I am forced to move from some cherished place. I've enjoyed every place I have ever lived, and every house I have ever lived in. Having built a home of my own on Grand Traverse Bay, I understand the special feeling that develops around real estate. But life is more than location, and homes are more than houses. Having watched people bond to walls and furniture, so as to become inseparable from them, I will work to see that similar idolatries do not manifest themselves in me.

Second, again concerning locations, I hope to live as long as possible in communities that welcome and incorporate people of all ages, interests, and lifestyles. I can't imagine choosing to live, go to church, or associate with nothing but 57-years-olds now. Why would I want to live, go to church, and associate with nothing buy 80-year-olds when I'm 80?

Third, while it is my expectation to live as independently as possible ... for as long as is possible ... I recognize that my need for independence will, sooner or later, be compromised by my need for security. I even understand the day will come when security issues may mandate some kind of assisted living or nursing home placement. I will be willing to go. For I know that one of the prime factors in having a good nursing home experience is the attitude of the one receiving the care. The quality of most nursing homes has as much to do with the people who live there as with the people who work there.

I also understand that others may sense my need for such a placement before I will. I will welcome that conversation. But I also know that such a conversation will go better if I initiate it. I will also keep in mind that it is unfair to avoid such places if it means asking other members of my family to take me into their homes. While not ruling out such a possibility categorically, I do not feel it fair to ask anybody ... no matter how close to me ... to surrender a significant portion of their freedom, just so I might maintain mine. I will never hold anybody's future as a ransom against my death. Nobody will ever have to wait for me to die in order to get on with the next phase in their life.

Fourth, I will fight becoming a victim. I will not allow myself to feel that I have been singled out for unfair treatment by God or any of God's underlings … including members of my family. I may, from time to time, feel that way. I may even slip and express such feelings out loud. But I will never allow those feelings to become my last word on the matter. For I know that the flip side of victimization is impotence … meaning that the degree to which I blame my fate on others (human or divine), is the degree to which I will forfeit the opportunity to manage what little of my fate that I can.

Fifth, if the opportunity presents itself, I hope that somebody will tell me I am dying. Keeping that information from me will not be considered an act of kindness. Dying is an experience. And you have heard me say before that I prefer to go through life collecting experiences rather than possessions. Why, therefore, would I chicken out on that philosophy at the end?

And while I hope to live as fully as I can, for as many years as I can … and while I would certainly not relish years of senility and suffering … I would just as soon have some time to come to terms with my terminal condition, as die from a heart attack in my sleep. Every time somebody dies suddenly and unexpectedly, someone else is sure to say, "What a wonderful way to go." Not for me, however. I would appreciate a little time for summing up, making amends and saying goodbye.

Sixth, I would rather be connected to people than machines.

The saddest thing about many of the nursing homes I enter is the way in which the residents withdraw from the world around them. Even those with the capacity to know better sometimes allow their world to become smaller and smaller … until it is no world at all. I abhor the thought. I trust that someone will fight to keep me in touch with who the president is, what the bishop is doing, and whether the Tigers are winning … not to mention the situation of the man in the next bed, the lady across the table, or the aide who comes to take my tray. And if, pray tell, my conversation ever becomes reduced to an enumeration of my bodily functions … how often I go … how easily I go … or my concerns about going … I hope that someone will verbally slap me silly and tell me (even at that advanced stage of my existence) to "get a life."

When the possibilities for "people connections" are gone, for God's sake … and for my own … don't keep me connected to anything mechanical. I do not find, anywhere in the Bible, where biological life is celebrated for its own sake. Biblically, the idea of creation means absolutely nothing apart from the idea of covenant. I take this to mean that life derives its primary meaning, and perhaps its only meaning, from relationships. Therefore, when people connections slip away from me, with no likelihood of their return, please don't connect me to anything else, either.

Barzillai (the Gileadite) had curried the favor of King David, who wanted to reward him. And who wanted to provide for him. But in declining David's gracious offer, Barzillai said (2 Samuel 19: 31-39):

Look, I'm old. I'm eighty. How many years are left in front of me? My usefulness is declining.

Can I discern what is pleasant from what is not?
Can I taste what I eat or what I drink?
Can I listen to the voices of singing men or
singing women?

Why should I be a burden to you, O King?
Let me die in my own city, near the grave of my mother and my father.

Fortunately, I can still discern what is pleasant from what is not. I can still taste what I eat and what I drink. I can still appreciate the voices of singing men and singing women. And I trust, continue to be more blessing than burden.

But such will not always be so. When it changes, let me go. As another preacher wrote:

There is a time to be born and a time to die.
A time to keep and a time to lose.

A time to embrace and a time to
refrain from embracing.

A time to speak and a time to butt out.

But death, which is my biological imperative, is also my theological opportunity. Maybe even my heavenly ministry. Jesus said, "Bill, I'll go get your room ready." So, the least I can do …

or maybe the best I can do … is do the same for you. It is the way of life. It is the way of faith. And it is the way of the Lord. Would you believe, dear Julie, a polka in the afterlife?

Bill's seventieth birthday, Fall 2010

September 14, 1997
First United Methodist Church
Birmingham, Michigan

Notes: Quotes from Tomas Lynch can be found in his book, The Undertaking: Life Studies From the Dismal Trade, published in 1997 by The Penguin Group.

These days, the best part of golf that Bill enjoys is watching his grandson, Jacob, as he grows into the game.

*Bill's granddaughter, Georgia, is both sweet and,
in her words, "fierce."*

Jacob Hopkins practicing on the driving range and breaking in his first set of clubs, gifted to him from his grandparents.

A super competitive soccer player, this is Georgia being fierce.

6

TILL MY TROPHIES AT LAST I LAY DOWN

One of my great present-day challenges is that my days of robust singing ... especially robust hymn singing ... are behind me. Also gone are my days as a First Tenor. How sad it is. But I still love hymnody including, to the surprise of many who know me, that section of the hymnal we often call "The Oldies But Goodies." The title for this sermon comes from that section. In addition, it is one of only two hymns written by a Michigan composer (the other being "Stand Up, Stand Up For Jesus.")

Scripture: 1 Corinthians 9:24-27, Philippians 3:12-16

Not that I'm obsessed with such matters, but I thought it important to tell you that exactly 79 hours from now, the world's greatest grandchild is going to turn two. Which is why his grandmother (the one I live with) and I recently took him to Disney World. If you need any further justification, chalk it up to yet one more item on my bucket list.

Jacob is a pretty smart kid. Already, there are a number of things that he and his grandpa can do. That list includes books, blocks, puzzles, trucks, and vacuum cleaners. Don't ask me how vacuum cleaners got on that list. I don't understand it either. The next stage I look forward to is board games. We'll start with something simple like "Candy Land." You spin something. You cover the spaces. You move up the board. Eventually, one of you reaches the finish line. Which introduces a question, "Do I let him win? And if so, how often?" I mean, if he never wins, he won't want to play. But if he always wins, he'll grow up thinking his grandpa is a stooge.

Besides, grandpa likes to win. Preachers are not supposed to say that about themselves. And, for years, I never believed that about myself. I always saw myself as good ole, easy going, Bill … play the hand you're dealt … take what comes with a grain of salt … don't get too high in victory or too low in defeat … because at the end of the day it's the experience that matters, not the outcome. Which self-description I shared one day with a few of my friends, leading one of them to say, "horse feathers." At least it kinda sounded like, "horse feathers." As in "Horse feathers, Ritter, you're one of the most competitive people I know. Because you play to win. And you usually do. Which has served both you and your churches very well."

Well, I didn't know what to make of that. I still don't. I think there's a world of difference between playing to win and needing to win. And it would appear that the Apostle Paul (an incredibly complex and enigmatic human being) thought so too. Paul seems quite comfortable using athletic imagery in his various letters to churches, never more so than here in First Corinthians …

> Do you not know that in a race the runners
> all compete.
> But only one receives the prize.
> So run in such a way that you might win it.

Later adding ...

> So I do not run aimlessly, nor do I box
> as if I were merely beating the air.

Back when I was leading recreation at Nardin Park UMC (as part of the "Tuesday Program" which also included choir practice and Bible Study), I found that where elementary-aged kids were concerned, if I could ensure a fairly competitive game by controlling who played on what team ... and if I could manage the game in a way that kept it close to the very end ... kids played hard, played fair, enjoyed themselves, enjoyed each other, and had a wonderful time. But if I let things get lopsided (or worse yet, one-sided), their interest waned, and their energy sagged. And if I introduced a game with no victory or defeat built into it, kids couldn't wait for it to be over. I also noticed that nobody seemed to mind losing as long as they thought they had a chance to win ... and played to win.

Winners get recognized. In Paul's culture, winners received a wreath made of laurel. In our culture, winners may receive dollars, ribbons, or a hundred other prizes in between. I teach preaching at Duke three months out of every year. I am in North Carolina every Fall, where Duke plays a major sport (football) poorly. Then I come back to Michigan ... cold and snowy Michigan ... just as Duke begins to play another major sport (basketball) brilliantly. And who among you has not seen a picture of Duke's basketball coach, Mike Krzyzewski, with all those gold medals draped around his neck after his USA team won the Olympic gold medal in Beijing last summer? Those same Olympics gave us Michael Phelps and his eight gold medals in swimming (even if the last one came as a result of his fingernail being a fraction of an inch longer than the fingernail of his chief competitor).

Yes, competition produces winners. And winners get trophies. I have made my peace with that, even though I understand it to be a system that, from time to time, produces its own share of pain. One of my best preaching students (in reflecting on her Swim Club childhood) said it was only years later when she learned that most of the ribbons and trophies she earned as a First and Second Grader and proudly displayed in her bedroom, were purchased by her parents.

But there is an even more sobering note to all of this. And you just sang it …

"… Till my trophies, at last, I lay down."

It's a strange phrase, really. Few of us understand it. Even though most of us love singing it. It comes from "The Old Rugged Cross," one of the few hymns ever written by someone from Michigan. Reverend George Bennard being his name. Reed City being his home. Pokagon, Indiana (where he was leading a revival) being the town. Methodist being the church. 1913 being the year. June 17th being the night. And Florence Jones being the first organist ever to play it (United Methodist Hymnal No. 504):

"So, I'll cherish the old rugged cross.
Till my trophies, at last, I lay down.
I will cling to the old rugged cross.
And exchange it some day for a crown."

One Saturday morning, the woman I live with asked me how my sermon was coming. She was not concerned with whether it was any good, but whether I was almost done. In short, she wanted to know if I was finished. And, if not, would I be willing to take a break from writing. She wanted to know if we could go look at some antiques ... across town ... way, way across town ... in a place she had read about that very morning.

So, applying a very small dab of polish to my oft-tarnished "good husband" badge, I said: "Why not?" For, while antiques are more her thing than mine, I tag along willingly, especially since she is married to one. But we often separate upon reaching a sale. Which is how I came to stand half-heartedly, that Saturday, staring at a huge table of trophies. Most of them had gold-colored figures mounted on brown-colored bases. There were hundreds of them. Some with names attached. Others without. Some with accomplishments itemized. Others without.

There were golf and bowling trophies.
Swimming and skating trophies.
Speaking and spelling trophies.
Singing and selling trophies.

There were trophies for a hole-in-one over here and a prize-winning carrot cake over there. I even saw a trophy for 20 new Fords sold during the month of January (more dust covered than

the others). There were medals too. And here and there a plaque. But in so far as I could tell, I didn't see any Oscars.

On each trophy was a little paper dot, the color of which provided a clue to its price. There were trophies for 25 cents, others for 35 cents. None of them cost more than half a buck. Heck, if I had laid down a fifty-dollar bill, I could have cleared the whole table.

But I found it kind of sad as I realized that the people who had once (in triumph) lifted them up had now (in death) laid them down. I pictured their families going through the house after the funeral ... sorting and claiming all the stuff. Upon arriving at the trophies, I pictured someone in the family saying to the siblings, "Any of you guys want these?" And when nobody did, I pictured them being thrown into a box marked "rummage" ... or "rubbish."

Who wants those old things? Well, we did once. At least I did.

I'll admit it. Gold stars. Blue ribbons. Lacquered plaques. Inscribed plates. Trophies and titles. I didn't mind them then. Truth be told, I don't mind them now. Not because there's a price on them. But because there's pride in them. Memories, too. That's because there's a little child in every one of us who goes around saying, "Did I do good?" And all that stuff hanging on the wall, sitting on the mantel, or pasted in the scrapbook says (whenever I sneak a peak at it), "Yes, Billy, you done good."

Occasionally, trophies get turned down. Even thrown down. There was the Swedish wrestler last summer who intentionally dropped his bronze medal, feeling that the judging decision had cheated him out of gold. So he was disqualified, stripped of the bronze, and ousted in disgrace. Apparently, as much as the world hates a sore loser, it hates a sore winner even more. All of which recalls the actor who, in turning down his Oscar, sneered, "I take great pride in being above such things."

No, if someone gives you a trophy, take it. There is nothing inherently wrong with it. Or sinful about it. Our church is not going to have a "Trophy Turn -In Day" … a period of spiritual amnesty where you are invited to trade old medals for pastoral absolutions. Hey, you earned it. You enjoy it. Just don't idolize it. Or allow yourself to become overly impressed by it. It was you then. It may not be you now. It tells the world what you once did. But it tells no one who you are now. Besides, while our trophies collect dust, you and I are dust. Which is why they get laid down shortly after we get laid down.

My favorite sports trophy is hockey's Stanley Cup. Because once you win it, your name goes on it. Better yet, you get to skate around the rink holding it. And, if you're a Detroit Red Wing, you get to parade down Woodward Avenue displaying it. Leading a columnist to write, concerning Detroit's spirited celebration with Lord Stanley's cup, that we were a bit excessive and unprofessional in our observance. Which led a Detroit editorial writer to counter that, "Only a writer from a town that had never won the Stanley Cup would bother to point that out."

But even our local balloon was punctured when Detroit Red Wing, Kris Draper's baby daughter was placed in the cup … undiapered … and let's just say that no champagne or beer was sipped from the brim that day. For, out of the butts of babes comes the reminder that even victories celebrated exuberantly, ought not to be taken too seriously.

To which Paul adds … "By all means, strive for the perishable wreath, but not at the expense of the imperishable one," which he later describes as "the heavenly call of God in Christ Jesus." How did we just sing it?

> *Till my trophies, at last, I lay down.*
> *And exchange it* (the cross) *and them* (the trophies)
> *Some day for a crown.*

I have never used payoffs in the future to motivate living for Jesus now. But, I do understand "pressing on." I do understand "straining forward." And I do understand "the upward call of Christ Jesus." But I understand them, not so much as heavenly prizes, but as earthly passions.

But since my time is drawing to a close, I trust you will excuse my ending on a note that is personal. I am no longer a runner who is going to win anything other than a free t-shirt. Frankly, I never was. And I never did. But one helpful thing I learned about running was this. Winners do not run to the tape. Winners run through the tape.

Which is the way I have always approached my ministry. Flat out. Full bore. Open throttle. Through the tape, not to it.

At my first retirement, I walked across the stage at Annual Conference and heard Bishop Keaton whisper to me, "You know, Bill, you cannot retire from a calling." From a task, maybe. From a job, maybe. From a church, maybe. From a career, maybe. From a profession, maybe. But not from a calling.

Paul Clayton recently identified three stages of retirement. The first he called go-go. The second, slow-go. And the third, no-go. Friends who suggest that I am flunking retirement seem clear (and mildly judgmental) that I am locked in the go-go stage of activity. Which is no longer true. For I sense that the song of my life is transposing itself into a lower and slower key. But the dominant chord of my melody remains ministry. As I suspect it will for years to come.

The late John Donne was once quoted as saying, "I date my life from the beginning of my ministry." I would not have understood that when I was twenty or thirty. I am not sure I understood that when I was fifty. But there is a sense in which I understand it now. Somewhere in time (as all those years slid by), I realized that what I did and who I was had become indistinguishable, one from the other. Which explains why I also date my life from the beginning of my ministry.

One of my lifelong heroes, Frederick Buechner, said it in tones soft and mellow …

Like anyone else pushing seventy-five, the stage I hold forth on is littered with the dead, including my only brother, my oldest friend, and an increasing number of others who I always assumed would be with me until the final curtain rings down.

In addition to that, my body is no longer altogether the one I have depended upon and enjoyed and neglected all these years, with the result that all sorts of things I thought I would be able to go on doing more or less indefinitely are slipping out of reach, and I am still young enough in my mind to bridle at it.

As I approach my seventy-eighth birthday, I know the feeling. I can't do what I once did, and many of the people I enjoyed doing it with are gone.

I find myself thinking about heaven, not a lot mind you, but more than I used to. For to me, heaven is more a promise that I trust than a place I can picture. But for me, heaven's lure is not because it promises endless extension … a life that goes on, and on, and on … but because it supports my hope for a blessed reunion. For I have loved and lost too many to envision it any other way. Hopefully, that reunion remains well out in front of me. But as for now, I take comfort that "the road taken" has been the right one. Which is why, at this stage of my life, I am simply staying the course.

May 2005
First United Methodist Church
Birmingham, Michigan

Notes: The quote from poet-preacher John Dunne can be found in Richard Lischer's book, Open Secrets: A Spiritual Journey Through a Country Church, Doubleday. The materials from Frederick Buechner can be found in his book, Speak What We Feel (Not What We Ought To Say), Harper-Collins.

7

WHY I STOPPED EXPLAINING HUMAN SUFFERING

If there is any preacher who does not have a sermon like this in the files, he or she had better write one. The entire message owes its outcome to a wonderful story by Peter deVries entitled The Blood of the Lamb, which has been around for more than half a century. But I sometimes wonder if I love it because it is so well written, or because (as a preacher and a father) I have buried too many children prematurely.

Scripture: Psalm 44:17-26; Romans 8:28, 31, 35-39

The story is told of a man who reached retirement and decided that, since he had more time to call his own, he would devote some of it to helping his wife. Specifically, he decided he would take on some of the cooking chores ... starting with the preparation of breakfast. Approaching the task with the zeal that made him such a success in the business world, he bought himself a little notebook and commenced to follow his wife around the kitchen … making little notes on her every action. Since he and his wife both liked oatmeal, his first lesson concerned the art of its preparation.

"Be sure to measure both the water and the oats," his wife instructed. "Use the small saucepan. Stir it while it cooks to avoid lumping and sticking. Don't forget to time it. Then, when it is fully cooked, turn off the gas and let it set up before serving. Once you are ready to wash the saucepan, soak it in cold water rather than warm."

Later, when her husband had gone outside to cut the grass, the wife looked in his notebook. Where, on the page marked "Breakfast," she read the following words: "Forget about oatmeal." Somehow, the explanation had overwhelmed the experience.

I must confess to a lifelong tendency toward explaining things. Much of my early ministry was spent offering explanations of religion. I believed then … and, to some degree, still do … that the gospel can be rational and (indeed) ought to be rational. Which is why I have tried, perhaps to a fault, to de-mystify the troubling issues of the faith. I have tried to explain what the Bible means … what the gospel says … what the church is … what the Kingdom requires … and what heaven promises.

But, in recent years, I have noticed a willingness to open my door to more and more mystery. When I confront a pressing problem, I am no longer a theologian with a bulldozer, but a pastor with a chisel … trying to hone down the rough edges of an issue, while realizing that I might never get it smoothed or solved. Lewis Carroll's caterpillar says to Alice in Wonderland, "Explain yourself." To which Alice replies, "I can't explain myself ... and neither can you." The self is a mystery. As is life. As is love. And so, I suspect, is God. Which does not suggest that we give up trying, but which does suggest that we succeed best when we begin by recognizing our limits.

High on the list of things I find hard to figure out is the reality and disproportionality of human suffering ... why it strikes ... why it hurts ... and why it is not spread out more evenly. If I were God ... which, fortunately, I'm not ... I'd do something about it. I'd make sure that those who loved me best, suffered least ... assuming (that is) that the distribution curve was within my control. It's the most natural thing in the world to think that God should look out for his own. I look out for my own. You look out for your own. I know that it borders on the edge of sacrilege ... and, perhaps, even heresy ... to admit to any of this. But while feeling such things may not be noble, it is normal ... even for the truest of believers.

Let me illustrate. Two Sunday mornings ago, when I was in Charlotte watching Duke demolish North Carolina ... which proves that there are times when divine justice really does smile upon the good and the godly ... you gathered here, in the snow, to praise God and hear Carl Price. And among those of you who gathered at 8:15 ... when the fattest worms are regularly distributed to the earliest birds ... were Paul and Alta Yager. Who, upon leaving the sanctuary, said, "Let's get ourselves some breakfast and then go see Letta Stevenson." Which they did, only to find that the people at Franklin Terrace had sent Letta to the hospital hours earlier.

So, Paul and Alta went to Beaumont Hospital ... found the emergency room ... found Letta's cubicle location ... and were within ten feet of Letta herself ... when (lo and behold) Alta hit the floor. Just like that. And when the outcome was pronounced, Alta had one broken toe and one broken hip.

By the time I caught up with Letta, she couldn't have cared less about what was happening to her. All she could talk about was what had happened to Alta. Three times she said, "I have but one question. And my question has but one word. And that word is, 'Why'?"

Now there are a lot of ways to come at the "why" of a broken hip. An orthopedic surgeon might answer it one way. A personal injury attorney might answer it another way. But Letta had little interest in whether Alta had brittle bones (which she doesn't) or whether Beaumont had slippery floors (which it doesn't). Letta wanted to know why ... in the wonderful providence of God ... saints (like Alta) on missions of mercy are not granted immunity.

And that question arose, not out of Letta's head. I mean, she didn't expect me to answer it (and given her 94 years of reading every study book and taking every Christian education class the church had to offer, she could have voiced the traditional answers better than I could). No, that question did not originate in Letta's head, that question originated in Letta's heart. For it was Letta's heart that harbored Alta's pain ... which far exceeded the pain of a few inflamed diverticulum, which was the problem that brought Letta to the emergency room in the first place.

Well, you might counter: "A broken hip is a mere blip on the radar screen of undeserved tragedy and pain." Until it is your hip. Or your blip.

Which it will be, sooner or later. That much is certain. Friday morning, I met Claire Beggs at the coffee pot. And, in my somewhat flippant style, I said, "How goes it, Claire, with your life and health and all things?" To which Claire answered, "I guess you could say I'm on top of the world." Ah, but the world has this funny way of rotating … so that one day you're on top of it, and the next day it's on top of you.

Many of you commented on my cover article in this week's Steeple Notes and upon Barbara Merritt's tongue-in-cheek recollection of being unable to feel the rumblings of a California earthquake, thanks to the magnificent suspension system of the car she called "Big Red" … a rented Cadillac Seville. Which led me to add, "I've spent a lifetime looking for a suspension system like that … one capable of smoothing out reality, eliminating bumps and minimizing vibrations from the outside world." Then I confessed to almost entitling my sermon, "Queen Mary Theology" … which would have had nothing to do with England's monarch or Jesus' mother, but with the cruise ship of the same name. On which I never sailed. But I have booked passage on more than one of her children. And what do they promise me?

> Come aboard our ship. We'll create a wonderful time for you. And we'll make a wonderful space for you. We are going to cross "The Deep," but you will neither know it nor feel it. And for those of you who are

nervous about it, we have inside cabins with no portholes. And for those who are still anxious, we offer center cabins. That way, you will never even feel the sway as we move across the formless voids and the unfathomable depths.

But I've heard of cruise ships where even the people in the center, inside cabins, got sick. Because nothing that was promised worked. And because the seas mounted an assault that could not be stabilized.

"Not on your cruise" … say you.

"At least not yet" … say I.

But it will happen, you know. And when it does, it will become your riddle to solve … or your mystery to accept. So what will you do when it is your daughter who dies … your son who is arrested … your home that is washed off the side of the mountain by the rains … your marriage that is broken into Humpty-Dumpty-like pieces that defy reassembly by all of the king's horses and all of the king's men (not to mention all of the king's psychiatrists and all of the king's preachers) … when it is your biopsy that comes back positive … your arteries that are determined to be 90 percent occluded … your business that is placed in Chapter 11 … or your Pastor-Parish Relations Committee that greets you warmly, all hands around, while humming in the background, "So long, it's been good to know you." When it's that real … and hurts that much … what will you do?

Well, some will turn from God. And I understand them. And some will turn to God. And I understand them, too. For when people speak to me from the valley, my initial response is to be accepting of anything they say. And there are times, if I let people be honest, when even those who turn toward God, do not do so kindly ... in that they have a bit of an ax to grind.

Every couple of weeks, someone sends me another list of "Bulletin Bloopers" ... things that were printed in church bulletins that just sorta came out wrong ... like the potluck supper that was advertised with "prayer and medication to follow." But the misprint I would share with you this morning was one that surfaced in the newsletter of a Lutheran church, which asked (in ten-point type): "HAVE YOU COME TO GRIPES WITH JESUS CHRIST?" To which the answer from the valley sometimes is: "Yes, I have ... and with his Daddy, too!" All of which is offered in the tradition of the Psalmist, who writes, "Why dost thou hide thy face from us, heedless of our misery?" (Psalm 44:24)

There are several explanations that theology makes to such folk. And there is some truth in all of them. But there is satisfying truth in none of them. Where traditional answers are concerned, no one answer fits everybody. And sometimes the sum of the answers combined won't fit one body; which leaves you out in the cold if that one body is you.

Let me be blatantly and painstakingly clear. You may deserve some of the stuff that happens to you. But you probably don't deserve all of the stuff that happens to you. What's more, I don't think God thinks you deserve all of the stuff that happens to you, either. In fact, I think that some of the stuff that pains you, pains God … and that some of the stuff that outrages you, outrages God … and that there may be occasions when God's "Why" is as anguished as your "Why" … and when the intensity of God's "O my God" rivals the intensity of your "O my God" … except for the fact that when God says it, God has no one to say it to but Himself.

Which is to suggest that God suffers too, don't you see? At least, I think He does. I mean, for me, the alternative is unthinkable. Does it sometimes hurt God to be God? Well, let me put it to you this way. Does it sometimes hurt you to be a parent?

Every four or five weeks, we say the Apostle's Creed. And what does the creed say about God? It says that God is "Maker" and "Father." And what does the creed say about the one God fathers? It says that he "suffered under Pontius Pilate, was crucified, died and was buried." Which had to hurt both Father and Son. And don't gloss over the hurt by saying, "Oh, but it was essential to our redemption" … or, "It was a mere pothole in the glorious road to Easter." Passion Sunday … which few churches want to deal with anymore … says that it hurt like hell. Or, as the little girl in my Confirmation class once said (in response to her first-ever reading of the crucifixion), "God, that's awful." And that's okay. Let it be what it is. Don't be in a great big hurry to clean it up. For, while the cross isn't pretty, it's far from the only thing that isn't pretty.

If I am not reaching you, let me give it one last try by telling you a story. Actually, it's not my story. Peter deVries is the one who tells it. It appears under the title, "The Blood of the Lamb." Some say it is fiction. But there are others who claim it is autobiographical. It is a story about a little girl named Carol. What a lovely, gracious, Christmasy name for a little girl. Carol is the only daughter of Don Wanderhope, which is quite a name in itself. For Don is something of a spiritual schizophrenic ... wandering between faith and unfaith ... between hope and despair. At issue for Don is Carol's health ... which is not very good ... and which is on the way to getting much worse. For Carol is battling leukemia and has reached the point where the disease, rather than the doctors, is expected to win.

But, like I said, this is not so much Carol's story as it is her daddy's. All of his inner conflicts meet, head on, on the day that he approaches Carol's hospital room with the birthday cake that he has had lovingly prepared by a local baker. But this is not to be Carol's birthday. This is to be Carol's death day. "She was taken," deVries writes, "from us dull watchers, on a wave that broke and crashed beyond our sight." Meanwhile, we are told that her father, "drew forth his handkerchief and, after honking like a goose, pocketed his tears."

After signing all the necessary papers ... and completing all the necessary notifications ... Carol's father adjourned to a nearby bar, where (after a few drinks) he remembered the cake. It was large and beautiful, completed just that very morning. There was a field of white frosting with Carol's name squeezed from the pastry bag in blue icing ... each letter carefully formed in flawless Palmer Method script. He had forgotten the cake in the church, leaving it on the back pew of Old St. Catherine's. Each morning, he stopped in the church to pray before going to Carol's room.

Returning to the church and finding the cake still in the same pew, he gathered it up in its wobbly box and began to leave. But let him tell it:

> Outside on the sidewalk, one foot on the bottom step, I turned and looked up at the figure hanging over the central doorway ... its arms outspread among the sooted stones and cooing doves. I took the cake out of the box and balanced it on the palm of my hand. Then, as if disturbed by something they saw in my eyes, the birds hurried into motion and flapped their way to safety across the street. Whereupon my arm drew back and let fly with all the strength within me. It was miracle enough that the cake should reach its target at all ... given its height from the sidewalk. And it was all the more a miracle that it should land squarely below the crown of thorns.

Now I suppose that a birthday cake smeared on the face of Jesus is something of a spiritual obscenity. But, on another level, it's a symbol of our complaint with a God who cannot save the Carols of our lives from the things that consume them ... corrupt them ... and ultimately kill them. But the blue and white icing was far from the first thing to mar the face of Jesus. For a closer look at the statue revealed earlier signs of pain and suffering that had been there forever. Finally, Carol's father, dazed by his explosion of anger, looked again at the besmirched face of the Savior.

> I seemed to see the hands free themselves of the nails and move slowly toward the soiled face. Very slowly ... very deliberately ... and with infinite patience ... the

icing was wiped from the eyes and flung away. I could see it falling in clumps to the cathedral steps. Then the cheeks were wiped down with the same sense of grave and gentle ritual, with the kind sobriety of one whose voice could be heard, saying: "Suffer the little children to come unto me ... for of such is the Kingdom of Heaven."

The Christian's answer to pain, don't you see, is really no answer at all ... but, instead, a magnificent gesture. Browne Barr suggests that the gesture is simply this: "that with grand and scandalous bravado, God leaves glory behind ... grandeur behind ... holiness behind ... heavens behind ... mountains behind ... to walk in the valley with the likes of us."

I may be saved by the fact that Jesus came to suffer **for** me. But I am moved ... sometimes to the point of tears ... that Jesus came to suffer **with** me.

March 21, 1999
First United Methodist Church
Birmingham, Michigan

Notes: Peter deVries story was published as a novel entitled, The Blood of the Lamb, It first appeared in 1961 and was republished in 2005 by University of Chicago Press.

8

SO IS IT REALLY TRUE: GOD WILL NEVER GIVE YOU MORE THAN YOU CAN HANDLE?

The sermon before you, compliments the one you have just left behind you, although it moves to a concluding argument, rather than to a concluding story. As one who re-preaches very few sermons, this one has probably seen the inside of a pulpit five or six times, including the pulpit of Duke Chapel at the heart of Duke University. But this version dates from July 16, 2006 at Epworth Assembly ... a lovely summer enclave on the shore of Lake Michigan.

Scripture: II Corinthians 11:24-27, II Corinthians 12:7-10, Romans 5:1-5

Once upon a time ... though not so very long ago really ... I had a pastor on my staff who regularly prayed aloud about pain, asking that those who suffered from it might be relieved from it.

But in order to make our awareness of pain more inclusive, that pastor subdivided pain into categories such as physical pain, mental pain, and emotional pain. Also mentioned, as I recall, was relational pain. To which you could add your own subsets, with social pain, international pain, and political pain being a few that come to mind. But his prayer was as appropriate as it was predictable, given that there is a lot of pain out there. And, as he was correctly assuming, a lot of pain in here, too.

Pain is a popular news story these days. At issue is the question of pain relievers. Specifically, should drugs that relieve it be made available for it, even though questions concerning dangers have surfaced? How much risk are we willing to accept in order to experience how much relief? When the subject is physical pain, the names that surface are Vicodin and Oxycontin. When the subject is metal and emotional pain, the spotlight turns to Prozac and Zoloft. And I am speaking to any number of you this morning who are taking, or have taken, one or more of the above. Meaning that you are far from indifferent to the outcome of the conversation. How much pain is too much pain? And how much will you risk in an effort to relieve it?

But there's a corollary question, isn't there? Probably a prior question. Namely, what's causing it? And sometimes the answer is easy and obvious … as in a pinched nerve. But sometimes the answer is less easy and less obvious … as in a crushed spirit, or a broken heart. Some causes being easier to find than others. And some causes being easier to fix than others.

But when there is no quick fix to the pain, we tend to link it with another word to describe the fact that it comes and stays rather than comes and goes. That word is "suffering" … as in "pain and suffering." If you are going to sue somebody, that's the phrase you employ. "You did this to me, leaving me with pain and suffering."

Not that anybody ever sued God. Although I don't know that for sure. Job certainly wanted to. And even got God to take the stand (as you will remember). But when God finished his opening statement (his four-chapter-long opening statement), Job recognized how unprepared he was in spite of how long he had waited. So he declined further cross-examination and simply said, "No further questions."

But why, you ask, would anyone sue God for pain and suffering? I suppose because God is often identified as being the source of pain and suffering. The Bible is full of people who figure that, where pain and suffering are concerned, God not only ladles it out but occasionally piles it on. Deservedly? Usually. But not necessarily. For, as Job contends, "I didn't deserve this." Leading his friends to say, "think again. Look harder. Dig deeper. You must have."

Job's friends don't come off very well in the Bible. "Who needs them?" we ask. "Nobody likes them," we answer. Truth be told, none of you even remember their names. Maybe we should have a little quiz this morning. I'll offer five pounds of coffee for anyone who can come up with the names of Job's friends. But heck, let's scrap the contest and save me the coffee money. Would you believe Eliphaz, Bildad, and Zophar? But if you read their testimony (which goes on for pages and pages), they were just trying to be helpful.

Which is what friends do, don't they? Try to be helpful, I mean. Especially when faced with pain and suffering. Your pain and suffering. Not knowing what to say, friends figure they are supposed to say something. And in "saying something," they would rather sound profound than trivial. So they introduce God into the equation, even though they are not entirely sure God fits into the equation ... of if God does, where God does. So they say any number of godly-sounding things like:

- "You may not understand it now, but someday you will see that God had a reason for this."

- "I know it's hard to lose a five-year-old, but God must have needed another cherub for the heavenly choir."

- Or, as I heard on Friday, a pastor told his parishioner that the reason her 21-year-old daughter was killed while doing a year of missionary service was so God could get the mother's attention about an unrelated matter. And when the mother asked why
God couldn't have communicated in a manner less dramatic (or traumatic), the pastor answered, "But my dear, you weren't listening. " Worse yet, the mother told me that story as if that were a normal thing for a pastor to say or a reasonable way for God to act.

I can go on and on with lines like that, spoken in funeral homes and hospital corridors, or printed on cards that are mailed out by people who find it easier to send something than say something.

Which I do not knock at all … theology being (at that point) secondary to friendship. For what will be remembered at the end of the day … or at the end of the siege … will be the effort made, not the theology expressed.

But I am amazed that many attempts to introduce God into the equation end up blaming God for the problem. Consider the phrase contained in this morning's title: *God Never Gives You More Than You Can Handle.* The intent being to instill confidence in your ability to handle things. As if to say, "Sure, this is hard. But you're up to it. You can do it. I know you can do it. We know you can do it. God knows you can do it. Otherwise, God wouldn't have given it."

To which I will eventually take exception. But not before commenting on a trio of underlying assumptions. The first concerns the word **"more"** (as in "God never gives you *more* than you can handle"). The word "more" implies that there are greater and lesser degrees of pain and suffering. Which may be true. Speaking personally, I have a high pain threshold. For years, I let them drill my teeth without numbing my mouth. I've been lucky, I guess. I have lived for 65 years with no serious pain … no prescription pain medication … no broken bones … not even a discomforting headache. And yet, there have been other days when I have been heard to grit my teeth and say, " It hurts. In fact, it hurts like hell."

Given the amount of time I spend in hospitals, I am often visiting bedside when somebody in a white coat asks somebody under the white sheet to rate their pain on a scale of 1 to 10. Which, given enough comparable data, most people can do. If yesterday's pain was a seven, today's might be a three. In fact, I recently heard somebody answer that question with the number 3.5. Talk about specificity. But it's all relative, don't you see. If the only pain you've ever felt is, objectively speaking, a one, it may feel like a ten ... because you've never known a ten. By definition, the first pain you ever feel is the worst pain you've ever felt.

I can't tell you how many times over the last eleven years someone has talked to me about suffering in their life ... disappointment in their life ... great grief and pain in their life ... occasioned by a great loss in their life ... and then, remembering that a dozen years ago Kris and I lost our son, Bill, to suicide, they will stop mid-sentence and say, "Of course, this is nothing compared to what you and your wife went through."

Well, I don't know whether it is or whether it isn't. What I do know is that to them, at that moment, whatever is bothering them feels about as bad as it can feel, and it hurts about as bad as it can hurt. So I never quantify pain (theirs being a 4, mine a 9). Neither do I minimize it. Pain's pain. That's what I tell them. Pain's pain. Meaning that the word "more" is relative, maybe even to the point of having no meaning.

My second concern is with the word "**handle**" (as in "God will never give you more than you can *handle*"). But I have discovered that handle-ability varies from person to person and experience to experience. Our ability to handle something is directly related to when it hits us, what we have undergirding us when it hits us, and (perhaps even more important) who we have around us when it hits us.

I have a pair of colleagues who are not only both clergy, but who are married to each other. While they were still in school, their first child was born physically handicapped and mentally impaired. Seriously so. After reading the book I wrote about Bill's death, the husband sent me an email recalling his son's birth some thirty years ago. Remembering that time, he wrote: "Ready or not; it forced us to grow up real fast." Which they did. But they knew of others who didn't. And I suspect they would be the first to say that there were moments early on … maybe even later on … when it was touch and go, even for them.

Which brings me to my third concern, this time with the word "**never** " (as in "God will *never* give you more than you can handle.) If that be true, then God miscalculates far too many times to be trusted. For the burdens people bear break the people who bear them far too often. Yes, breaking points vary. But I have discovered that most of us have one. Which is why I do not believe God ever introduces suffering into someone's life as a means of testing them. Because, far too many fail the test.

Sure, some suffering will test us. Sure, some of us will pass with flying colors. Sure, some of us will be better for it, wiser for it, more understanding and compassionate for it. Sure, people (like bones) will heal stronger at the very place where the break occurred. But there is nothing automatic about that. And while God can help that to happen … will help that to happen … wants more than anything for that to happen … God does not know that will happen, nor can God assume that will happen.

Pain's pain. Handle-ability varies. Everyone has a breaking point. Which brings me to the most critical word in the sentence.

"God never **gives** you more than you can handle." Actually, I'm zeroing in on two words here, those being the words "**God gives.**" So let me say it right out. Where pain and suffering are concerned, I do not believe that God is in the distribution business.

The Bible is full of suffering. And the Bible is full of people who wish God would bring suffering into the lives of others (especially the "sic'em" Psalms ... "O, God, those guys treated me poorly, treated my mama poorly, treated my people poorly, so it would please me to no end if you would blast them into smithereens.") What the Bible is not full of is people asking God to send more suffering their way. Paul, as we read earlier, boasts in his sufferings, actually listing them (complete with numbers) in his letter to the Corinthians. Five floggings, Three beatings, One stoning, Three shipwrecks, Thirty-nine lashes. Ever in danger from rivers ... from bandits ... from Gentiles ... and from false brothers and sisters. Cold, hungry, and naked, to boot. And (I love this): "Under constant daily pressure because of anxiety from my churches." Not to mention the "thorn in his flesh" that never went away, in spite of multiple pleadings that God make it go away.

But Paul stops just short of laying this off to God's doing. Over and over again, Paul says: "God can use this." But Paul skates very carefully around the suggestion that "God caused this."

In the Romans passage, Paul again boasts of sufferings ... suggesting that suffering has toughened him up and taught him how to endure without losing hope. In effect, Paul is saying, "God has helped me come to terms with suffering even to the point of finding peace in the midst of it." But never does Paul say concerning it: "I have been singled out by God for it."

From time to time, when a couple gives birth to a child that is less than perfect (and, sooner or later, all children will be less than perfect … but I am talking serious limitations here, birth defects here, mental impairments here, life-expectancy boundaries here), friends will go to the Hallmark store in search of just the perfect card to send them. And the card selected will often suggest that, faced with the need to find the perfect parents for such a challenged child, God searched high and low until he selected them.

Which, at first glance, feels like a tremendous vote of affirmation for those parents. Which is how it was meant. And which may be true. Those parents may indeed be perfect. And if not, God may work to make them perfect. Years later, they may even say, "That child was the best thing that ever happened to us." After which they will describe everything from lessons that would have never been learned or love that would have never been shared had that child never been conceived. Although it may also turn out that the birth of that child soured the marriage, split the family, broke the home, and created lifelong problems for the child and the society onto which the child was thrown.

For all I know, those parents may be perfect for the job. And, even if they aren't, God may empower them for the job. But I do not believe God starts out with a quota of already compromised children to place and then goes looking for people with whom to place them. And my second reaction, were I to receive one of those cards and read that God thought my wife and I were perfect for the challenge, would be to say, "Does that mean if we were less so, our child would have been more so … perfect, I mean?"

•••••

My friends, life is filled with hard and painful challenges. As to why they come in the number they do, and the magnitude they do, to the people they do, I do not know.

Concerning those people, some bear up. Others break down. Those who bear up, gladden God. Those who break down, sadden God. God loves all of them … seeks to help all of them … would never do anything to hurt any of them … and (I believe this with all my heart) never *did* anything to hurt any of them.

Where pain and suffering are concerned, God is not in the distribution business. Can any of you really hear God saying:

- A little for you … you can't handle it.
- A lot for you … you can handle it.
- A medium amount for you … you may or may not be able to handle it.

Again I say, God is not in the distribution business. So what business is God in? That's too big a question for too short a time. But I owe you something. So, for starters, let me try this. Where pain and suffering are concerned, God is in the sharing business.

One day, I happened upon God and thought I would tell him about my boy. Whereupon …

God listened.

God cried.

God put his hand on my shoulder.

And then God did a very strange but truly wonderful thing. God put his hand in his back pocket, took out his wallet and, flipping through those little vinyl jackets, said, "Bill, I've got a picture I want to show you."

July 16, 2006
Epworth Assembly
Ludington, Michigan

9

THE ELEPHANT'S BALLET

While reading this sermon, you will encounter the sentence, "life is not just about acquiring; life is also very much about relinquishing." When I wrote it in 1987, I was talking to others … parents, colleagues, and friends. Today, 2018, I am talking to me. Which means that this sermon now speaks to me in ways it never could have twenty-one years ago. I am grateful to Deb Prasad who lobbied to include this sermon in this book. She was right. But the ultimate judgment, dear reader, will be yours.

Scripture: Corinthians 12:1-10, Galatians 4:12-20

I trust that you have read my notes on the cover of this morning's bulletin, in which I describe the musical oddities of a one-woman handbell solo and a one-man band. Such performances owe more to agility than they do to artistry, while allowing the question, "How in the world do they do that," to obscure the more interesting question, "Why in the world would anyone want to?"

While talking about such things at our staff coffee break on Friday, Ross Pomroy told us about a pair of performers who regularly appear at the "Bavarian Fest" in Frankenmuth. Apparently, they not only perform together, but are married to each other. She plays the cowbells and sings. He plays the accordion and yodels. According to Ross, they aren't that bad ... especially later in the evening. But, as I said in Steeple Notes, the amazing thing is not the perfection of the performance or the quality of the artistry. What is amazing is that such a thing can be done at all.

Which brings me to Bob Kemper. Bob is a Congregational minister who I have good reason to admire, but have never had an occasion to meet. Bob has written his autobiography and entitled it, *An Elephant's Ballet.* The title is more than a little strange. But no less curious is the fact that Bob chose to write his life story at a much younger age than I am currently. Still, it is worth calling to your attention for one simple reason ... that being that Bob Kemper is functionally blind, and the "elephant's ballet" is the metaphor he uses to describe his situation. The first sentence in his book reads: "Bob Kemper is like an elephant doing a ballet. It may not be a very good ballet, but it is amazing he can do it at all."

What a fascinating image Bob has chosen. For the ballet is generally considered to be a symbol of elegance and grace (as in the picture of Rudolf Nereyev pirouetting at center stage). What the ballet is not is a dance one commonly associates with elephants.

I do not often share lengthy third-person stories in sermons. But this one is both well told and timely. For while few of us will necessarily lose our sight, most of us will (over time) lose something. Life is not just about acquiring. Life is also very much about relinquishing. To be sure, all of us are cruising toward the "big loss." But on our way to the "big loss," most of us will lose lesser things. We will lose good jobs and old friends. We will lose youthful innocence and middle age confidence. And we will inevitably lose things like body parts ... and functions ... and vitalities ... and capacities ... not to mention potencies.

Which is why Bob's story is more than mildly instructive. For at the age of thirty-six, Bob Kemper was on a roll. He had known fruitful ministries. He had received critical acclaim. And he had just been named editor of a newly launched journal entitled, *Christian Ministry.* He was in great demand as a public speaker and freelance writer. What's more, he had a wife and three kids and had just purchased a home in the same Illinois town where he had previously served as an associate minister. Who could ask for anything more? It felt like "moving up" and "coming home" at one and the same time.

The change, when it came, was neither swift nor easy. It didn't happen all at once. Instead, it happened bit by bit, punctuated by doctors, clinics, exotic optical machinery and long slow periods of waiting. His first symptom was double vision, compounded by a lack of clarity in dim light. Soon to follow was the loss of sight in the center of his left eye. One doctor led to another, with each new appointment requiring endless repetitions of the same tests. Eventually, what they all showed (and confirmed) was that blood cells around the macula were hemorrhaging, depriving the eye's thin membrane of nourishment and cleansing. Which, in turn, produced scar tissue of the kind that would not permit the passing of light. Cells were effectively being destroyed, with no way of regenerating them.

His doctors performed laser surgery to halt the spread of the degeneration and to save the sight in his other eye. It worked, for a while. He worked, for a while. During that period, he began describing himself as the Sammy Davis, Jr. of the clergy. It was descriptively appropriate … for about six months. Then the same process started in the other eye … leading to the same doctors … the same tests … and the same surgical attempts at containment. After which came the bad news: "You are functionally blind. The damage to your central vision is irreparable."

But doc, what do I do now?

Bob, you learn to live with it.

The resultant loss was double. It was the loss of sight, followed by the loss of self-esteem. Bob Kemper did not think well of himself, feeling both inadequate and angry because there was virtually nothing he could do as well as he used to. Looking for someone to blame for his pain, he began to flare at his wife and kids, while distancing himself from old friends attempting to be helpful. During that period he wrote: "An angry elephant with a shriveled-up ego can feel very sorry for himself."

Even his attempts at adjustment created fresh problems. He received an adequate disability allowance from Social Security, only to discover that if he tried to work for pay … even a little bit

... his benefits would be nibbled away, meaning that one of the few things he could do to help his pride ended up hurting his pocketbook.

Eventually, he was directed to Chicago and some new technological innovations for the blind. For the first time in eighteen months he read a newspaper, with the print magnified forty times its normal size and positioned in the line of his peripheral vision. He learned to accept being driven, thus gaining mobility. He learned to use cassette tapes, thus gaining access to libraries. He learned to memorize sermons, thus gaining access to pulpits. He even tried writing again in little bits and spurts.

One day a Congregational church he had previously served as an associate found itself between pastors. They said, "Come preach for us in the interim." So he did. But the interim never seemed to end. The search for a new pastor became interminable. But few seemed to care. That's because attendance was increasing. And more than an occasional parishioner could be overheard saying, "Too bad we can't just keep Bob. We could do a whole lot worse, you know." Then one day they up and decided, "they could just keep Bob." Except that when they offered him the job, he turned it down ... writing in his rejection letter, "This congregation needs something more than an elephant that can do a passable ballet for a couple Sundays."

But the day he refused the job was also the day he turned the corner. For he now had to face something other than his blindness. He had to face his evasion. And he had to admit that his most immediate handicap was not with his eyes, but with his spirit. He had begun to think of himself as a handicapped preacher, rather than a preacher with a handicap. He wrote: "I had allowed myself to become an elephant, and had indulged myself in thinking that this lousy ballet was (and would be) my only accomplishment. I had made a cage of my problem … moved into it … and (worse yet) grown comfortable there. The one thing I had never forgiven myself for was for not being perfect."

Having finally come to that understanding, he asked the church if they would be willing to reconsider him. They did. But he told them to make no contractual concessions to his blindness. They didn't. Instead, they called him as their pastor. He said, "Yes." For all I know, he is still there today.

But in the spirit of his saga, allow me to raise a trio of truths. First, it is truly amazing that elephants can do the ballet at all. It is amazing that blind guys can serve churches. And it is amazing that people can yodel the Lord's Prayer while playing the hand bells with one hand and an accordion with the other.

Most of us, you see, never venture such things. That's because we are cursed by visions of perfection remembered … visions of perfection imagined … or visions of perfection projected (far out of reach). That's what Bob Kemper was saying when he wrote, "In my anger, I had never forgiven myself for not being perfect." He could not do the things he once did, or as effortlessly as he once did them. Which hurt. But when you can't accommodate yourself to such facts and make the appropriate concessions that will enable you to go on living, you are going to travel further and further down the road from discontent to misery.

If perfection is the only measurement of self we will accept, you and I are in a race we can't win. For our bodies will fail us. Our capacities will decrease. Our energies will diminish. Death will steal others from our midst. And then ... a step at a time ... a day at a time ... or an ounce of strength at a time ... it will steal us.

But what a ballet we can perform in the interim, if only we can negotiate a truce with our limitations. I hate to see people victimized by remembered glory. I hate to see people stopped in their tracks by their fear that ... as ballets go ... theirs may not amount to much. And I especially hate to see kids "quit" on things, having barely started them, because they figure that they'll never get to be good enough, fast, enough.

One of the things I hate about playing golf with new partners is the way I find myself standing on the first tee, making all those stupid excuses as to why I'm not very good. For I realize that I am not so much making excuses for myself, as to myself. But whoever said I had to be a great golfer (or even a moderately good one) before I could enjoy hitting golf balls. So now, upon approaching the first tee, I quietly give myself a little speech. Which goes something like this:

Just shut up, Ritter and stand there ... club in hand ... looking at what an incredibly beautiful day it is. Notice how lush and green the fairway is. Observe how blue and cloudless the sky is. And calculate how lucky you are to know even three people who like you well enough to put up with your company for eighteen holes. So just stick your tee in the ground ... put your ball on it ... and then rear back and smack the damn thing some place. And give thanks to God for the privilege.

Sometimes I'll play golf with an older fellow. He'll step up there and hit one nice and sweet, straight down the middle. Whereupon he'll turn and say, "Pretty good for an old guy." And I like that. Because that's not an apology. That's simply an honest acceptance of his limits, and an honest appreciation of what can be done within them.

Consider the Apostle Paul. Moments ago we read about his ongoing battle with an infirmity he called his "thorn in the flesh." It permeates his Corinthian and Galatian correspondence. But nobody knows what it was. What we know is that it not only ailed Paul, but also embarrassed him. We also know that, on more than one occasion, it drove him to experts (who failed to cure it). We know that whatever his "thorn in the flesh" was, it was both visible and offensive to other people. We also know that Paul did not resign himself easily to it. Three times he prayed to the Lord, "Get rid of this." Yet Paul also thanked the Galatians for their sensitivity to him, as when he wrote: "Though my condition was surely a trial to you, you did not scorn or despise me." In fact, one commentator on this passage said, "Paul handled his affliction in such a way as to turn it into an asset in dealing with the people of Galatia." Maybe they looked at Paul and figured it truly was amazing that this elephant could do the ballet at all.

Which leads to my second truth (which is almost the flip side of the first). Nowhere does it say that elephants are required to be proficient in ballet. We fall into the trap of saying, "The only way people will consider me to be a good elephant is if I learn to do a reasonably graceful ballet. Or the only way people will value my presence, is if I can sing ... dance ... run around in circles ... jump through flaming hoops ... meet my weekly quotas ... double the number of members ... even as I leap moderately tall buildings in a single bound."

But the problem with basing our self-esteem on our productivity is twofold. First, we can't keep it up forever. And second, we end up missing the affirmations that come our way in the interim (even in response to ballets we perform that are less than perfect). Remember that Bob Kemper rejected the first offer made by the church. It was a wonderfully affirming initiative on their part. So why did he turn it down? Because in his own mind, he hadn't perfected his blind ballet. Therefore, he couldn't believe that anybody else could be entertained or inspired thereby. But he was wrong. People could. And they said so. It was his own fault that he couldn't hear them.

And the third truth is simply this. Ballet is not so much a dance that elephants do for the benefit of an audience, as a dance that elephants do in the company of their friends. Friends are those people who will laugh with us rather than at us ... and who will shed (on our behalf) ten tears of sympathy for every one tear of pity.

Most important, however, is the fact that friends are people who will tell us the truth. Bob Kemper wrote, "All along, people were honest with me ... even when I couldn't be honest with myself. Doctors. Family members. Friends. No one tried to pretend that I did not have a problem (and a real one), even at a time in my life when I was still making that pretense. Over time, I came to realize that my best friends were those who would tell me the truth, with their honesty serving as my greatest single source of support."

Somewhere in the middle of Bob Kemper's odyssey, he was visited by a friend suffering from a similar form of blindness. But what the friend told him proved to be a genuine shock. "Bob," he said, "the condition we share is not so much a tragedy as it is a bother. It's kinda like going bald. There's really not all that much we can do about it."

"Wow, was I angry," said Kemper. "Here my whole life was coming unglued, and he's comparing blindness to baldness (first your hair falls out ... then your eyes fall out). But, in a way, he turned out to be right. For I had to learn what he had learned ... that my loss was not the most important thing in my life ... and that I could not allow it to become my primary defining characteristic."

We would never think beginning a conversation with someone new by saying, "I'm bald, you know." But how many of us launch similar disclaimers by saying, "I'm functionally blind, you know ... that's who I am ... so don't expect too much from me ... and if you don't think much of my ballet, here's why."

But we don't have to apologize our way through life. And we don't have to wear our disclaimers on our sleeve every time we go out in public. We are not dancing to an audience. We are dancing with our friends.

So hark, my friends. I hear music in the distance. Rise, elephants. Let us be dancing. Sure, an elephant does a lousy ballet. So do you. So do I. But a late-breaking rumor out of New York has it that Rudolf Nureyev can't preach for beans.

July 23, 1995
First United Methodist Church
Birmingham, Michigan

Note: Dr. Robert Kemper died at the age of 75 in July of 2010. He served as senior minister for the First Congregational Church of Western Springs, Illinois (1973-1998)

10

APPOINTMENT IN SAMARRA: MIDDLE OF THE NIGHT MUSINGS ON THE SUGGESTION THAT "TO EACH OF US IS APPOINTED A TIME TO DIE"

During fifty years of ministry, I have found that things that keep me awake at three o'clock in the morning often trouble others as well. This sermon falls in that category. Is there really a Book of Life kept in Heaven? And, if so, is my name in it (and are there any dates written beside it)?

Scripture: II Kings 20:1-11

Back in my novel-reading days ... to which I will probably not return until I glide (or somebody pushes me) into retirement ... I kept company with an author named John O'Hara, who wrote about the "social set" living in the mythical town of Gibbsville, Pennsylvania. Critics have suggested that O'Hara's signature novel, Appointment in Samarra, was one of his best. Oddly enough, it begins with a 14-line quote from W. Somerset Maugham. Listen:

> There was a merchant in Baghdad who sent his servant to market to buy provisions. In a little while the servant came back, white and trembling, and said, "Master, just now when I was in the marketplace, I was jostled by a woman in the crowd. When I turned, I saw that it was Death that jostled me. She looked at me and made a threatening gesture. So lend me your horse, and I will ride from this city and avoid my fate. I will go to Samarra. Death will not find me there."
>
> The merchant lent him his horse, whereupon the servant mounted it and dug his spurs in its flanks. As fast as the horse could gallop, he went. Then the merchant went down to the marketplace and saw the woman standing in the crowd ... the same woman who had frightened his servant. Approaching her, the merchant said: "Why did you make a threatening gesture to my servant when you saw him earlier this morning?" "That was not a threatening gesture," she answered, "it was only a start of surprise. I was astonished to see him in Baghdad, for I have an appointment with him tonight in Samarra."

The woman (of course) is Death ... with the assumption being that you cannot avoid or outrun her if she has decided that the hour of your appointed rendezvous is now.

This idea (that "Death is a stalker who refuses to be denied") seems to fascinate everybody. But it especially fascinates teenagers who pay good money to see Death do her thing (his thing, somebody's thing) in horror films galore. Where teenagers are concerned, the bloodier, the better. One such film, Final Destination, opened Friday (although I haven't seen it and have no plans to). The headline in the local review read: "Teen Gorefest Takes a Predictable Path."

As for the plot, it concerns a high school French class and two adult teachers who board a plane for Paris ... and a field trip to die for (pun, clearly intended). Just before buckling in, one of the students has a premonition of the plane exploding, moments after take-off. In a panic, he blurts out his grisly vision. All of which leads to a fistfight and his expulsion from the aircraft. This is followed by the voluntary decision of a few others ... and one teacher ... to similarly deplane. Sure enough, the plane takes off, and the plane blows up ... killing the second teacher, the remainder of the class, and everyone else who just happen to be on board.

But that's only the beginning. One by one, the lucky ones (those who got off the plane in the nick of time) die too ... in a very specific order. What is the message? That Death will not be cheated out of his victims (notice, here, that Death is identified with masculine pronouns rather than feminine ones). To reveal any more will spoil your fun ... should you go. Which I recommend you don't. And the chances are good that you'll never see this film as an in-flight movie selection. But your kids and grandkids will take it in, and may even echo the sentiments of one of its stars who said, "Sure, you can't take this too seriously. But it's a fun ride. Plus, it's got the best deaths of any movie I've seen. That, and it's scary." Lord, save us.

This is certainly not a new idea. If memory serves me correctly, Emily Dickinson once pictured Death as keeping its appointments by carriage. Which, as an idea, is certainly more refined. And which bears some relationship to "the chariot" (and its accompanying "band of angels") that some would sing is "coming for to carry me home."

Images? Of course, they're images. Are they meant to be taken literally? I doubt it. Are they meant to be taken seriously? I'd suggest it.

There's a line of progression in all of this, is there not? Death calls. Death comes. Death collects. Death carries. But does Death stalk? And is there a time … prescheduled … for Death to appear? I think not. But there are many who do not agree with me. Including my maternal grandmother who, as I am sure you know, was once a major force in my life. Since she lived to 97 … I almost said "the ripe old age of 97," but the last few of those years were anything but "ripe" … you could hardly say that my grandmother was cheated out of her innings.

But a couple of years prior to her death, she was absolutely convinced her time had come. She was in the hospital. I can't recall the reason. There didn't seem to be the usual signs that Death's door was open … or even slightly ajar. But she thought it was. So she told all of us in the room she loved us, was proud of us, wished the best for us, and said "good-bye" to each of us (by name, no less). Then she folded her hands on her chest and quietly closed her eyes. Which was lovely. And touching. But somewhat premature.

Which led her to conclude that the "Man Upstairs" (her term, not mine) either wasn't ready for her or didn't want her. Whereupon, she would ask me to ask Him (meaning the "Man Upstairs") what was going on. My grandmother was not overly religious. But she was convinced that death came by pre-appointment. And she was further convinced that somehow, through some heavenly screw-up, she had missed hers.

I have heard smokers tell me that they feel no need to quit, because "when your number is called, it won't matter whether you have spent your life sucking on pure oxygen or sucking on Pall Malls."

I have heard skydivers say, "not to worry" in discussing their risky business, given their contention that "when your time comes, it won't matter whether you are falling through the clouds or snoozing on the sofa, you're history." And "until your time comes," you haven't got a reason in the world to worry.

I have heard soldiers speculate that the difference between coming home to a victory parade or coming home to a funeral procession is a simple matter of whether there is a "bullet out there with your name on it."

When Bobby Phills, star guard of the Charlotte Hornets, was pulled dead from the wreckage of his roadster a few short weeks ago, one of his teammates said (in a eulogy, no less), "that God called Bobby home early" … somewhat overlooking the fact that

Bobby was driving his roadster in excess of 100 miles per hour when God's call came. Sometimes it amazes me when I hear the things God gets credited with ... or blamed for.

Are our days numbered? Most assuredly. "We are born to die," the Bible says. We are "like grass" ... which has its day in the sun (or its season in the sun). Then, as is the case with grass, either time withers us or life mows us. Whereupon, life (at least as we know it here) goes on without us.

Early on, the Bible talks (allegorically, methinks) about a few people who celebrated an incredible number of birthdays. I mean, where did they find birthday cards that read, "Congratulations on your 600th?" But with the passing of years, the Bible pretty much settled in on "three score and ten" (meaning 70), or "four score" (meaning 80), as a normative number for the human lifespan. Still, it bothered biblical writers that there were some who died prematurely ... meaning early ... and they didn't quite know what to make of it. After all, what is the Book of Job if not a speculative discourse on the question of why some things do not seem fair ... or just ... or right?

Clearly, the Bible wrestles with the idea (I almost said, "plays with the idea," except that it sounds too frivolous ... and Lent is certainly not a time to be frivolous ... that when the curtain comes down, God's hands can be found on the pulleys. Which is what we have in today's little story about the near death ... followed by the 15-year reprieve ... of King Hezekiah. His story is really old. It dates from between 705-701 B.C. (making it more than 2,700 years old).

God tells Isaiah (the prophet) to tell Hezekiah (the king): "Get your house in order. For you shall not recover." Whereupon Hezekiah weeps and prays, telling God that he has always "talked the talk and walked the walk" where belief in God is concerned. Which apparently cuts the mustard with God. So God intercepts Isaiah (who has not quite reached the middle court of his exit from the palace) and says, "Halt. Go back. Retrace your steps. Reverse your message. Tell Hezekiah I have heard his prayers, I have seen his tears, and he's right. He deserves more time. So I'll add fifteen years."

Which is exactly what happens. Isaiah turns around and tells the king the good news. He also heals Hezekiah's boil with a "figgy poultice" (we must be talking "virulent infection" here). Then Isaiah adds, "The sign that you have been reprieved will be the shadow's retreat on the sundial by ten intervals." Whereupon Isaiah cries to God, and the shadow retreats ten intervals on the sundial. Message sent. Message authenticated.

It's a fascinating story. But why did I choose it for today's text? Because, on the one hand, it suggests the notion of a predetermined date with Death ... as in "now" ... or "fifteen years from now." But it also suggests (as early as 700 B.C.) that nothing is set in concrete, that everything is negotiable (or amendable), and that while God has appointed for each of us to die, the circumstances of our dying (including the timing of our dying) may also have something to do with us. Indeed, quite a bit to do with us.

When Jesus says to the rich fool (the guy with so much "stuff" he can't find sufficient barn storage in which to keep it) that "this very night your soul is being demanded of you … and what will become of all this stuff then," I don't think Jesus is so much predicting as he is preaching. And when Jesus says, concerning himself, "that the Son of Man must suffer and die," I am one of those who believes that the real temptation of Jesus (indeed, the last temptation of Jesus) is that he could have slipped from supper … slipped from Jerusalem … slipped quietly back to Galilee … become a fair-to-middling country preacher … retired at 65 … wintered at a Red Sea resort … and died of congestive heart failure in his bed … had he chosen to exercise his will at the expense of his Father's.

In short, I believe there is some "play" in the system, and that death neither stalks us nor consults a fore-ordained appointment calendar as to when it should visit us. As concerns the listing of my name, I do not think there is a number beside it. And as concerns the listing of yours, I do not think there is a number beside it, either. As to the possibility that "angels of death" may come (and I'm extremely comfortable with the idea that they do … quite apart from the television series), I think they come to take us home, not to do us in.

Does God know (in advance) that death is near? Darned if I know. I suppose it depends on what you mean by the word "advance." I doubt that God knew "in advance" that Bobby Phills was going to die in that fatal car wreck in Charlotte … although I suppose a certain predictability of tragedy can be attached to behaviors such as driving 105 miles per hour on the city streets of Charlotte, rather than on the oval track at Darlington. So God "could have known" … just as many of us could have known. It's relatively easy to be prophetic when the people you are prophesying about are stupid.

As concerns the premonitions of death that come to some from time to time, I simply do not know what to make of them. I hear the same stories you do ... stories about people who never had a sick day in their lives (and haven't seen a doctor in years) who suddenly, with no apparent explanation, start putting their affairs in order. All the while, they deny they are doing so. But then they die. And everybody says: "They must have sensed something."

Did God send them a message? Or were they unconsciously listening to their own body language and intuiting self-sent signs of their own mortality? Again, darned if I know. But if you force me to take a position, I'll lean toward the latter rather than the former.

Now I know ... I just know ... that some of you are going to hit me at the door with the doctrine of predestination ... or the idea that all things are pre-determined by God, to the point of being pre-scripted by God. We'll have to talk about that someday, you and I. Suffice it to say, for now, that I don't embrace it. And I know relatively few Methodists who do.

Prior to St. Augustine (354-430 A.D.), the early church never preached this. And when it does appear in theology, it is never in the context of who dies or who lives, but who is saved and who is not. At issue in the doctrine of predestination is not whether our daily comings and goings have been pre-planned, but whether our salvation has been pre-assured. Unfortunately, the doctrine has been perverted to say things it never intended to say. Which is probably why Augustine said it should never be preached in the hearing of common folk. So much for my "history of doctrine" lecture.

Dinner with dear friend and pastoral colleague, Dick Cheatham, who confirmed and enhanced much of what I know about St. Augustine.

•••••

One final word! From time immemorial, preachers have seized upon the unpredictability of death's timetable as a way of warning the faithful and the unfaithful to "clean up their act." "You never know," the preacher thunders, "it could happen any day … any time … any place … to any one of you" (funny, I never hear them say "to any one of us"). Still, it's a legitimate sermon topic, given that John the Baptist made a career out of it. Even Jesus preached it from time to time ("Fool, what if all the chips get cashed … the IOUs get called … the chickens come home to roost … this very night?").

But I am among those who feel that if obedience to the gospel is beneficial to the next life, it must be beneficial to this one. Why obey? Because it's a better way to live … a happier way to live … a healthier way to live. The Bible is clear. There is no way of living that will deny death. But there are some ways of living that may delay it ("may," not "will" … there are no guarantees). But which leads me to say that the best reason for cleaning up your act … the best reason for getting religion … the best reason for turning to God … the best reason for coming home to Jesus … is not in case you die. But in case you don't.

March 19, 2000
First United Methodist Church
Birmingham, Michigan

Note: The narrative concerning Hezekiah and Isaiah can also be found in the first 22 verses of Isaiah 38. I chose to read it from II Kings, given that the flow of the narrative is tighter and more sequentially organized in II Kings. Most scholars suggest that Isaiah's version has certain key elements misplaced. However, Isaiah's version also includes Hezekiah's "psalm of gratitude," alleged to have been uttered in response to the 15-year reprieve. The "psalm" is a lovely piece of writing but probably existed, quite apart from Hezekiah's voicing it, as a psalm popular in the liturgy of the Temple. The quote from Somerset Maugham is taken from the opening page of John O'Hara's highly acclaimed novel,

Appointment in Samarra, published in 1934 by Harcourt Brace and renewed in 1961 by Penguin Books.

As concerns horror movies that earn the title, "gore-fest" because of their bloody and grizzly deaths, let the record show that significant portions of Wes Craven's film Scream Four were filmed in my daughter's kitchen.

11

REMEMBERING WILBUR

Some may find it strange that I have included this sermon in this collection. After all, it is highly personal and geographically specific. But, like mine, not all families are tightly knit. And many have a missing person in them … for whom nobody ever looks.

Scripture: Luke 12:1-7

Everybody loves a good family reunion story. I mean a "real" family reunion story. I am not talking about those annual gatherings where everybody brings a dish to pass, and there are games for the youngest, ice-cold watermelon for the oldest, prizes for those who came the farthest, and the "annual listing" of those who have been hatched, matched and dispatched "since we assembled last." To be sure, those reunions are lovely. My wife comes from a family that does one every year … down Springfield, Ohio way. And we go every few years, whether we need it or not. Because whether we know it or not, we do.

But those are not the kinds of reunions that interest me today. Instead, I want to talk about the coming together of people who have been apart a much longer time … some by choice, others by accident. War came, and they got split up. Conflict came, and they split themselves up. They lost touch with each other. Then they lost track of each other. They didn't know where the other one lived. Then they didn't know if the other one lived. May have cared. May not have cared. Who can say? Then one day there was a reunion. Orchestrated or accidental. Painful or tearful. Brothers, reunited after 50 years. Parents and children who hadn't seen each other since birth, seeing each other now. A strange voice on the phone. A strange face at the door. "I bet you don't know who I am. And after hearing who I am, if you tell me to go away and never come back, I will. But I'm …"

I like reunion stories. I suppose because I hear so many of the separation variety. I heard three in the last week. I heard of a son, living in the same town, out of contact with his mother for more than five years. A daughter who hasn't seen her daddy since the day of her wedding. A brother who didn't come to the funeral. Could have. Should have. Didn't want to. Flat out refused to. I hear such stories every week. I hear them from you … although these three didn't come from you. Trust me.

None of this is without parallel in the Bible. While the people of Israel preached family solidarity … and while the stories of Israel undergird what we commonly refer to as "family values" … the Bible is full of families that went their separate ways and may (or may not) have gotten it back together before "time and chance happened to them all."

Abraham and Lot. Jacob and Esau. Joseph and his many brothers. Amnon and Absolom (David's boys). The brothers in the Prodigal Son story. They all took off and went their separate ways. As did lots of others. To be sure, there are fewer Bible stories of women splitting up and taking off. But, then, there are fewer Bible stories of women, period. What's more, economic dependency in a patriarchal society tended to keep women closer to home ... and closer to each other. Still, stories abound of the first wife forcing the exit of the second wife. And who can forget the older sister who stole her younger sister's husband on her wedding night (with the aid of a conniving father and much-too-much wine)? I can go on. But to what end? Inch for column inch, there is more in the Bible about family squabbles than about family values. It has never been easy to care for kin ... at least, some kin. For, while blood may be thicker than water, it is not necessarily sweeter than wine.

Kindly allow me to illustrate. I do not come from a large family. Neither do I come from a particularly close family. My mother was an only child. My father was one of four. But all four are dead. And the other three never had children. Meaning that I have no cousins. My only sister died, a few days before I came here. But she did leave me with a pair of nephews. Fortunately, I married into a larger collection of people. Otherwise, the "family" portion of my Christmas card list would be satisfied by buying one box every three or four years.

Which brings me to Wilbur. An unusual name, really. I haven't baptized a Wilbur, ever. I don't know any Wilburs, now. And apart from the TV actor with the talking horse (Mr. Ed), I can't say that I ever recall many Wilburs.

But Wilbur was my uncle. Let me explain. Earlier, I said that my father was one of four. Fred, his oldest brother, was born in 1900 and died (while still living at home) in 1946. I was six years old. I remember Fred's dying. But I do not remember Fred's funeral (leading me to suspect that I didn't go). Which was a bad decision on somebody's part. Six-year-olds should go to funerals. But that's not the way things were handled then.

Wilbur followed Fred, born in 1906. And in 1909, there came the twins, George and Marion. George was my father. He died in 1967. Marion died shortly thereafter. And from everything I knew ... or thought I knew ... Wilbur was long gone before either of them. Meaning that I haven't had a reason to use the word "uncle" or "aunt" for a long, long time. As best as I can recall, I last saw Wilbur in 1953 when his father ... my grandfather ... William C. died. I was all of 13. And by that time, I was deemed old enough to go to funerals.

Until the late 1940s, Wilbur, like Fred, remained single and lived at home. Then, for reasons long buried in history, he took off for the Upper Peninsula where he met an older woman in Negaunee and married her. Her name was Pearl. And the only two things I remember about Pearl were that she had a loud, shrill laugh and that she cooked every summer at our Methodist camp in the Upper Peninsula ... the one called Michigame.

Wilbur and Pearl reappeared in Detroit at the time of his father's funeral. Whereupon they moved into his mother's house, overstayed their welcome (in the mind of his younger sister, Marion), got into it with somebody (probably Marion), and left in a huff, never to be seen again. When his mother died, six years later, Marion simply informed the rest of us that she had attempted to locate Wilbur and that Wilbur was dead. Which everybody accepted ... and nobody questioned. Truth be told, nobody really missed him. Wilbur was a loner ... an odd loner. His father used to call him "the governor." When I once asked my grandfather why he called Wilbur "the governor," my grandfather said, "Because he knows everything and thinks he's always right."

This spring ... 48 years after I last saw Wilbur ... my wife was on the Internet doing some genealogical research. Suddenly, a dangling thread of information danced across the screen. Following it, she learned that Wilbur died ... not in the '50s ... not in the '60s ... but in 1992 in Iron River, Michigan. Which first surprised me. But then saddened me. Clearly, I never found him. Largely because I never looked for him. But, in part, because he had no interest in being found. So what to do?

A month or so later, we made a few phone calls and researched a few records. We got Wilbur's death notice from the Iron River paper. We talked to the fellow who arranged for his funeral and the lawyer who settled his modest affairs. Then, on the day before the Fourth of July, Kris and I left our vacation house in Elk Rapids and crossed the bridge into the Upper Peninsula.

Iron River is at the far end of the peninsula ... past Manistique ... past Escanaba ... past Iron Mountain ... past Crystal Falls. It is a town that mining left behind ... but that Wilbur found. Why he went there, I don't know. But he settled in there. Initially, he lived at the county fairgrounds where he mowed the grass and handled the maintenance. Eventually, he bought a house. Then another. And a third. And in 1992, following Wilbur's death,

Back row (left to right): Fred Ritter, Wilbur Ritter. Front Row (left to right): William C. Ritter, Marion Ritter, Helen Ritter, and George Ritter (Bill's father)

those three houses (combined) sold for the grand total of $2,500.

Early on, Wilbur put Pearl in a nursing home and walked to see her every day until she died in 1968. Then, for 24 more years, he rented out his houses … delivered the Iron River paper … sold a few Watkins products … and made lawn ornaments and windmills out of orange crate wood that he salvaged from the local supermarket. While at the market, he met Tony Fittante, who stocked the shelves (as one of the three jobs that kept him going). In Wilbur's declining years, it was Tony who gave him rides, delivered his groceries, kept him company, and ultimately arranged his funeral.

Kris and I had lunch with Tony and thanked him for the attention he paid my uncle. Tony said, "I wish we had known more about him. We never knew he had family … never knew he once lived downstate … never saw a picture (or heard a story) of anybody from his past." It hurt to know that he never acknowledged us. I can only surmise that he never missed us. I suppose you could say that he disappeared. But the word "disappear" would imply that somebody, somewhere, took note and gave search. Sadly, we never did.

Upon learning that I was clergy, Tony told me about one of his other jobs that involved cleaning the Catholic church in Caspian. Then Tony added, "Your uncle used to stop by and talk with the priest from time to time. And I know he said his prayers. But I don't think he was a Catholic."

Then, as we were leaving lunch, Tony added, "Have you gone to Joe's? You've got to go to Joe's. Most every day, your uncle stopped by Joe's." So I said to Kris, "Do you think we should go to Joe's?" "Why not?" she said. So we did. As you have probably surmised, Joe's is a tavern. You can find it on a street of houses in an old, old section of town. Joe is dead now. His widow, Katie, runs the place. She lives upstairs. Every day, she opens up about noon and closes between six and six thirty. Katie is well into her eighties and is missing more than half her hearing.

There were a few tables and a few stools. There was also a black and white TV (which "the regulars" say last worked in 1961). And there is really nothing for Katie to sell except pop in cans and beer in long-necked bottles. But of the ten people there at 2:00 pm on the Fourth of July, at least eight of them knew Wilbur. Except they knew him as Bill Ritter (his father's name … my name). And they got a big kick out of one Bill Ritter coming to look for another Bill Ritter. They told more stories about my Uncle Wilbur. I learned about the only luxury he ever had (a Chevy Impala he drove when he first came to town). I learned about the wagon he pulled on his daily rounds, once the Impala was history. I learned about the school kids who made fun of him, not so much because of his beard, but because of his rigidly erect posture that made him look like Abe Lincoln. And I learned that some folks thought he was secretly rich because he mistrusted banks and was known to carry his savings in his sock.

In appreciation for all those stories, I bought a round for the bar … pushing a twenty dollar bill in the general direction of Katie. I figured I'd have to supplement it some. But after serving ten beers to ten guys on ten stools, she gave me a ten and five back as change. When I pushed back the five, she told me I could come back anytime I wanted … a sentiment that was roundly echoed by "the boys" as Kris and I bid farewell and walked out the door. As for going back, one wonders if we ever will.

So why tell you this? Three reasons. All of them short. As for sweet, you tell me.

First, I guess family is where you find it ... where they know your name ... tell your stories ... recognize your wagon ... buy your papers ... deliver your groceries ... arrange your funeral ... and inform your preacher/nephew (when he shows up 40 years too late) that you said your prayers. I left, feeling as if Wilbur had been adopted by an entire town. And while I didn't have the faintest idea why he had decided to become an orphan in his middle years, I am glad that, in God's great providence, there were people who took him in. Could it be that "blood" is vastly overrated?

Second, blood does count for something. So, if there is anybody who is as lost from you and yours as Wilbur was lost from me and mine, look for them. Make an effort. Pick up a phone. Write a letter. Activate the Internet. Do something. I know you've got a million reasons not to. And if you tell those reasons to the guy on your right, the woman on your left, the usher in the narthex, the person pouring punch in the parlor ... even if you tell them to me at the door ... we'll listen to the reasons for your neglect and find them compelling. But I have this funny feeling that God will listen to your reasons and find them stupid. How do I know that? Because my understanding of the gospel is that "God was in Christ, reconciling the world unto himself, and entrusting to you and me this ministry of reconciliation." Which means that every reason we offer for sitting on our hands, probably strikes God's ear as a little bit stupid.

Third, if God really knows names ... if God really numbers hairs ... if God really takes note of falling sparrows (which is beyond my comprehension, but what do I know?) ... then no one ever completely falls through the cracks. I forgot Wilbur.

Wilbur forgot me. But I suspect that God remembers us both. And in God's good time ... if not in either one of ours ... I think there will be an opportunity to get it healed. So I'll just keep an eye out for somebody pulling a wagon who looks like a governor ... or, better yet, President Lincoln.

July 22, 2001
First United Methodist Church
Birmingham, Michigan

12

TWILIGHT TIME

Having written about my uncle in the previous sermon, I turn now to my mother. But, in a broader sense, it is really a sermon about aging and decline. I preached it the Sunday after she died ... mercifully so ... in August of 2002.

Scripture: Psalm 71; II Corinthians 4:16-18

Eight and a half years ago, in the pregnant stillness that characterizes this sanctuary on Christmas Eve, I told you of my mother's birth. It took place in New York City in July of 1915. She was the first child born to Agnes and Anton Meyers. Her last name should have been Markuzic, but my grandfather changed his name at Ellis Island, figuring that "Meyers" sounded less foreign than "Markuzic." My grandfather came from Slovenia (northern Yugoslavia) as a young adult. So did my grandmother. But they didn't come together. Neither knew of the other in what they referred to as "the Old Country," though they could have, so few were the miles that separated their villages.

My grandmother left her village when she became a teenager. Her departure followed the death of her mother. It was either leave or go to work making bricks for her father (alongside her brothers). Instead, she hired out to a family in a nearby town to cook, clean and take care of children. Having done it there, I guess she figured she could do it anywhere. Which is why she said "yes" to an inquiry from a Jewish jeweler and his wife (surnamed Rubinstein) who lived in a New York City apartment overlooking Central Park. "Cook and clean for us for six months," they said, "and we'll pay your passage to America." So she did. And they did. Which is how it came to pass that in one of her rare nights off in the "Big Apple," she met a fellow countryman named Anton in a restaurant frequented by Slovenians. He thought she was beautiful, whereupon he gave her a nickel and sent her off to buy a pail of beer.

My mother was the offspring of their union. Now living as a threesome across the Hudson River in New Jersey, they received an overture from the Rubinsteins. "We'd love to see the baby," they said. "Why don't you bring her 'round come Saturday next … in the afternoon … for coffee and cake?" So they came, ate and showed off the baby. And as they rose to go, Mr. Rubinstein removed his checkbook from the inside pocket of his suit coat and said. "You are young. You are just starting out. Your whole life is in front of you. You will have many children. My wife and I will never have children. We can give much to your little girl. Let us adopt her from you. In return for which we will pay you. In fact, we will pay you whatever you ask."

And while my grandparents took no offense at the offer, they refused the offer. And, as far as I know, they never heard from the Rubinsteins again. That little girl was Lillian (Markuzic ... Meyers ... Ritter ... Brear). She was my mother. And she was the only child my grandparents ever had. Now, 87 years later, she is dead. When I told that story to Rabbi Sherwin Wine of Birmingham Temple (just last week when we co-officiated a wedding the day before mother's funeral), he looked at me in genuine amazement and said, "My gosh, Ritter, you could have been me."

Religiously speaking, that was as close as Mother ever came to being Jewish. But she never came all that much closer to being Catholic, either. Most Slovenians were. And still are. My grandparents went when they came to Detroit ... to Mass, I mean. My mother made her First Communion. And my grandmother took the basket containing Easter dinner to be blessed by the priest. But they were far from faithful. And one Christmas Eve, when the priest told all the C and E people to get up and give the regulars their seats, my grandfather muttered, "We're outta here." And they were. Forever.

Which was why all my mother knew when she met my father was that the church she was staying away from was the Catholic Church. Of course, all my father knew when he met my mother was that the church he was staying away from was the Lutheran Church. Which was how it came to pass that, needful of a clergyman to marry them, they approached a Methodist who was serving a church known for giving popcorn to little children.

He married them ... sans popcorn. And he baptized me ... again, sans popcorn. The need to take me there got my mother there. And she joined, the same Sunday I was confirmed some 12 years later.

My mother's early years were not what she would have called happy. She didn't much like being an only child. Neither did she like being a Slovenian immigrant. And being poor didn't make things any easier. Nor did marriage to a very giving man (my father) with a very unforgiving addiction (alcohol). To be sure, there were good times and good memories. Musically inclined, she played the piano, taught me to love and appreciate music, and relished her years in the church choir (several, as a soloist). Economically speaking, she did what she had to do when she had to do it, to make sure that we ate (and had other essentials during the years of my father's decline).

And truth be told, it was her job that saved her. She loved going to work at the J. L. Hudson Company. It gave her esteem as well as employment ... friends as well as food money. And one of them (the friends, I mean) became a special part of her life. Indeed, he became a special part of all of our lives when he married her 20 years and 25 days ago. His name is Harold. He is here today. And there is no question in my mind that the "Harold years" were her best years. That's because there was no question in her mind that the "Harold years" were her best years.

Well, not all of the best years. We (Kris and I) could see her dementia descending six or seven years ago. Harold saw it five years ago. If mother ever saw it, she never said it ... except for that moment a couple of weeks ago when she whispered to my wife, "What's happening to me?" Her only verbal concession to decline was her repeated pronouncement, "It's tough to grow old." But by the time she asked Kris what was happening to her,

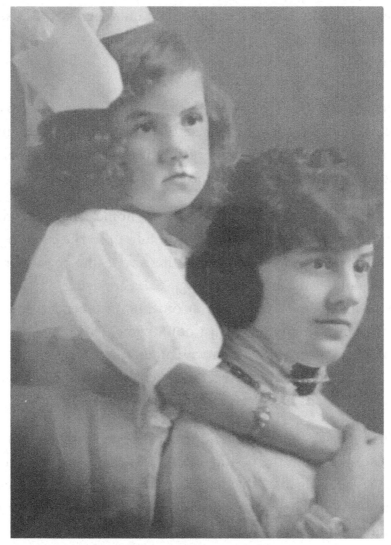

Bill's mother, Lillian Ritter and Bill's grandmother,
Agnes Meyers.

everything was happening to her … dementia, cancer, stress fractures, a stroke, loss of mobility, loss of stability, multiple falls, ugly bruises and the shingles. It wasn't the least bit pretty. But considering what could have been, it was mercifully short. Seven weeks can seem like an eternity when you're living it. But seven weeks constitute a mere season of suffering, once you move beyond it.

Hospitals helped. Hospice helped. A small but ranks-closing, circle-the-wagons family helped. For Kris and myself, more friends than anybody has any earthly reason to deserve, helped. And for Mother, morphine helped.

A splendid surprise was having Julie home. Harvard behind her. California before her. She left on July 14 so she could report on July 28. But three-quarters of the way to the coast, her cell phone rang. It was her boss saying, "Sales are dying. Stock prices are falling. Don't come now. Come in October instead. Go somewhere. Go anywhere. Just don't come here." So, she came home. She arrived just when we couldn't have done it without her. Do you call that fate? Fortune? Serendipity? Spirit? You tell me. Theologians speculate. Fathers appreciate.

Circling back to my mother, I think she would say (concerning her life) that both the best and the worst came late. Sort of like pro basketball games that don't really heat up till the fourth quarter. Which is worth remembering in this youth-adoring culture of ours. Roger Wittrup asked me the other day if I realized that the only time in our lives when we like to get older is when we are little kids. When you are little, you are so excited about aging that you think in fractions. "How old are you?" "I'm four and a half." Have you ever heard anyone say they were 36 and a half (or 61 and 11/12ths)?

You get into your teens, and you tell people, "I'm gonna be 16." You could be 13. But, hey, you're gonna be 16. Then one day you become 21. Great word, "become." It sounds like "arriving." Which it is. But then, nine years later, you turn 30. Which makes you sound like sour milk … he "turned" 30.

After which you are "pushing 40." Notice how uphill that sounds. Eventually you "reach 50" … which is language commonly associated with the word "stretch." Finally you "hit 70." It sounds like a collision.

Well, when Mother hit 70, I think she would have chosen the verb "cruise" rather than the verb "collide" to describe the experience. And even if she didn't speak it, she was probably on it. A cruise, I mean. Like I said, it was as good as it ever was in those years … and for several years beyond.

Not that she could sustain it. Or control it. That's where life differs from Chevys. There's no cruise control. Life slows down. We slow down. It's sort of like my golf game every time I ring up three or four good holes in a row. What happens? The wheels come off, that's what happens. What then?

Well, the better question might be: "Who then?" In answer to which the psalmist might say, "God, then."

> From birth, I have relied upon you,
> You brought me forth from my mother's womb.
> I will ever praise you.
> You are my strong refuge.
> Do not cast me away when I'm old.
>> And do not forsake me when my hair is gray
>> and my strength is gone.
>>> *Extracted from Psalm 71*

The Apostle Paul is even more graphic in his description when he tells the Corinthians:

> So we do not lose heart.
> Though our outer nature be wasting away,
> our inner nature is being renewed daily.
> For this slight momentary affliction is bringing about
> an absolutely incomparable abundance of glory.
>
> Which is why we find ourselves looking,
> not on those things that are seen,
> but on those things which are unseen.
>   *II Corinthians 4:16*

All of which leads to a trio of thoughts. First, if you believe that it takes one to know one, Paul (himself) must have been in a pretty serious state of decline when he wrote those words.

Second, it takes more detachment than I can muster to describe my mother's decay as a "slight momentary affliction." But maybe that's why Paul stands at the apex of the apostles while yours truly is a mere peon of a preacher.

But third, I join Paul in believing that there are "unseen things" to see, which are more the result of God's good gift than our good glasses. I have told you this before, but 38 years of attending the dying tells me that the closer we get to the end of this life, the thinner the membrane that separates this life from whatever follows this life. And I think that that membrane (while never fully pierced on this side of the grave) is sometimes stretched so thin as to be momentarily transparent.

Allowing us to see what? Darned if I know. But permit me some guesses.

A vision, perhaps ... of a world that is brighter, fairer and safer (especially safer) than the world that is painful and passing.

At the beginning of the service, we belted out a hymn. Don't you just love hymns you can belt? And don't you just love the word "belt?" The title, "Are Ye Able." The author, the late Earl Marlatt. Earl Marlatt was the Dean of Boston University's School of Theology. He wrote at least one other hymn that I know. We shall sing it momentarily. It's not in our hymnal anymore. But it should be. He wrote it near the end of his tenure as Dean of B.U ... when weariness was upon him and weakness, within him ... when ascending Commonwealth Avenue (which isn't very steep) was becoming more and more of a chore. Giving rise to the final verse:

> Spirit of life, at evening time
> when weary feet refuse to climb,
> give us a vision, eyes that see
> beyond the dark, the dawn and thee.
>
> *No. 462 United Methodist Hymnal*
> *(1964 Edition)*

Ah yes, a vision, perhaps ... **perchance of God**. A young boy and an old man are sitting on a dock in the late afternoon, fishing. They are also talking about many things, like why sunsets are red, why the rain falls, why the seasons change, and why girls are so weird. Finally, the boy looks up at the old man (who is, at that moment, busy baiting his hook for him) and asks: "Does anybody ever see God?" To which the old man says, looking across the blue waters, "Son, anymore it's getting so I hardly see anything else."

Finally, I believe (at twilight time) **that some of us may see others of us.** Not those here. But those there. Who, for my mother, may have included her mother, her father, my father, her daughter and our son. And leading me to pray, "Whatever else you have planned for me, dear God, please don't let me be lonely."

The last time I was convinced that my mother could hear me, I prayed with her (as I have prayed with hundreds):

O God, none of us knows where the road goes.
We don't know when it goes up.
Neither do we know when it goes down.
We don't know when it crests the mountain
    or plunges into the valley,
Or when it rounds the bend where no one here can follow.
All we know is that we do not walk that road alone.

Then I said to my mother, "If you can hear me, take my hand. It's about three inches in front of yours. You're going to have to reach for it." And she did. That was Sunday.

Three days later ... on Wednesday ... I could have sworn I heard God tell her the very same thing. You may doubt that. But I'll bet my mother's life on it.

August 25, 2002
First United Methodist Church
Birmingham, Michigan

Lillian and Harold on their wedding day in 1982.

Note: The sermon title is taken from a ballad, much recorded across the last half-century. While I haven't researched its origins, a lot of people credit it to The Platters in 1957. Truth be told, I think it's older.

The story about the young boy and the old man on the dock comes courtesy of John Killinger in a book entitled Christ and the Seasons of Ministry, published by Broadman, 1987.

As concerns things that can be seen through the "thin membrane," see my treatment of this theme in my sermon entitled "Visions of Wrigley Field on a Saturday Afternoon" (September 28, 1997). A lot of people are talking about the "thin membrane," none more profoundly than those who trace their devotional roots to Celtic spirituality.

13

OUT OF SEASON

Not everybody dies when they are old. Some leave us early, "being done too soon" as Neil Diamond used to sing. The death of Cherie DeRose from a pulmonary embolism while she was still in her thirties, rocked an entire church. What follows is my effort to address the grief that was spreading, like a funeral pall, over a 1,700-member congregation.

Scripture: Ecclesiastes 3, verses 1-8.

INTRODUCTION:
(The following remarks were shared with the congregation immediately prior to the reading of the scripture.)

The sermon you will hear this morning is not the sermon posted on the signboard or printed in the bulletin. That sermon, "On Playing To Win," will probably not appear until late November. It is a good sermon. It is a nearly-prepared sermon. It is a sermon on a subject that interests me greatly. But it is not a sermon that is appropriate for this morning.

As many of you know, Cherie DeRose died suddenly in the wee hours of last Thursday morning. Cherie wore a number of hats at Nardin Park, causing her to be widely known and dearly loved. Some knew her as Ed's wife. Others knew her as Katee, Lindsay, and Merrill's mom. Still, others knew her from Family Fellowship, Vacation Bible School, and whole host of activities related to children.

The words "a Cherie DeRose Production" came to be synonymous with no small number of Family Life events, including hot dog roasts, all-church picnics, and talent shows. Each September, Cherie was the lady who led us on a bear hunt.

What you are about to hear is not a eulogy for Cherie DeRose. That comes tomorrow. What you are about to hear is not a recitation of the great resurrection promises of our faith. That comes tomorrow. What you are about to hear is not a reminder that even those things that appear momentarily defeating shall nonetheless be swallowed up in victory. That comes tomorrow. Instead, what you are about to hear is an attempt to take seriously the things we are feeling and the questions we are raising, knowing that both the feelings and the questions have a certain timelessness about them that goes far beyond the present hour and far beneath our personal pain.

In that vein, let me read the oft-quoted cadences of the book of Ecclesiastes, Chapter 3, Verses 1-8.

For everything there is a season
and a time for every matter under heaven;
a time to be born, and a time to die;
a time to plant, and a time to pluck up what is planted;
a time to kill, and a time to heal;
a time to break down, and a time to build up;
a time to weep, and a time to laugh;
a time to mourn, and a time to dance;
a time to throw away stones,
and a time to gather stones together;
a time to embrace,
and a time to refrain from embracing;
a time to seek, and a time to lose;
a time to keep, and a time to throw away;
a time to tear, and a time to sew;
a time to keep silence, and a time to speak;
a time to love, and a time to hate;
a time for war, and a time for peace.

SERMON:

Shortly after I came to Nardin Park, George Swan called and invited me to play golf on a winter Sunday in January. Knowing George's fondness for the Carolinas, I figured we were going to Pinehurst. No such luck. We were going to Brighton. Or, more specifically, to Lakeland Country Club, near Brighton. That's where George plays during the summer when he isn't pulling teeth. But, January?

Yes, January! They had chipped holes in the ice crust, marked off a course, shoveled the fairways down to a thin layer of white stuff and given us a bunch of orange balls to hit. It was cold. It was fun. It was confusing. It was ridiculous. I think they even had prizes at the end. It was the kind of thing that enabled you to go to work the next day and say, "Guess what I did over the weekend?" But I don't see it as something that will catch on.

For in Michigan, golf is a warm-weather sport. Skiing is a cold weather sport. Everybody knows that. Die-hards, aficionados, and other idiots may try to stretch the seasons of each. But if skiers want to hit the slopes in June, they fly north. And if hackers want to pitch and putt in January, they migrate south.

Very few things are questioned if done in the proper season. But violate too many seasonal boundaries and people will begin to look at you oddly. Some boundaries are rigorously fixed by the calendar, like the boundaries of deer season. You had better not shoot a deer 30 minutes too early or 30 minutes too late. Other seasons are calendar-focused, but not calendar-locked. Such is the Christmas season. Everybody knows the final date, but nobody can tell you how soon is too soon to begin getting ready.

Some seasons are defined by the calendar, some by climate, some by the legislature, and some by the economy. But, in most cases, seasons are defined by tradition and practice, as each culture develops a common consensus as to what "feels right." If a teenager becomes pregnant, we grieve for her situation, believing that there is time to be a child and a time to have a child. If a 19-year-old basketball player signs a contract worth several million dollars, we shake our heads in dismay. Something about such a contract seems "untimely." We figure that he either hasn't earned it, won't have the maturity to handle it, or lacks the capacity to appreciate it. There are certain rhythms and pacings to life, which we hate to see violated. We caution gardeners who rush the season because we know what late frosts can do to early blossoms. And we caution gardeners who stretch the season because we know that Mother Nature can't be fooled forever.

Such are the lessons that come with growing old and wise. You need to have been around the track a few times before you sense that there seems to be a time for everything. You don't know exactly why. And you don't know exactly who, if anybody, set it up that way. But, after a while, you begin to feel the rhythms in your bones ... summer and winter ... seed time and harvest ... work and play ... waking and rest ... spending and saving ... fixing up and starting over ... making love and making pasta.

"To everything, there is a season," suggests the ancient writer of Hebrew wisdom. And generations ever since have said, "Yea verily," or "do tell," or "preach it," depending on the style of affirmation that feels comfortable at the time. Actually, we don't know the old sage's name. We don't know much about him. We don't know what occasioned his writing. And, if we read very far on either side of these beloved lines, we find him to be a bit of a dour pessimist. But, as one commentator suggested, "these few verses about times and seasons are all we know about the book of Ecclesiastes, and all we really care to know." The author probably sat down one day and said, "This is how life feels to me." And upon reading his words, a lot of us said, "This is kind of how it feels to us, too."

"To everything, there is a season; and a time for every matter under heaven." It doesn't say when that time is. But most of us have a pretty good idea of when it ought to be. For, over the years, we have quietly observed the seasons in their passing. As long as things follow the script with which we have become comfortable, we are not prone to raise a quarrel.

On Friday morning, in order to put an hour's worth of distance between ourselves and the events of the week (and in order to enjoy another unseasonably spectacular November day), Kris and I went walking through Heritage Park. We didn't talk a great deal. We held hands a little more tightly than usual. We often stopped to look at the woods and the water. Occasionally a breeze would pick up, triggering another tumbling of leaves from branches. In the spotlight of the sunshine, the leaves slowly danced their way to earth. There they joined millions of multi-colored comrades who had already surrendered and given up the ghost.

With thoughts of this sermon very much on my mind, I watched the leaves more closely than is my nature. How natural this all is, I thought. This is November. This is the season when leaves should do this. Leaves fall in the fall. I learned it years and years ago. I may lament it. But I don't question it.

But were the leaves to fall in spring, that would indeed surprise. I would take it as a sign of something being seriously wrong. I would search for someone who could tell me why. Given my botanical ignorance, I would not pretend to know. My hunger for knowledge would, however, be more than a simple lament. Of course, I would miss the leaves. That goes without saying. But underneath my "missing" would be my fear that whatever had happened was somehow terribly and unexpectedly wrong.

My grandmother is a tough old leaf, still clinging to the tree in the late December of her years. She'll be 97 years old on the twentieth of January. She lives in a nursing home, comfortably now after a contentious beginning. She still thinks ... pretty well, talks ... pretty well ... and interacts with her environment ... pretty well. Having ascended the pecking order of power (yes, even nursing homes have pecking orders of power), she has the bed nearest the window (and nearest the bathroom). She still prides herself on the fact that nobody has to do anything for her. That's not entirely true. But it's helpful mythology, so who am I to disturb it? She cannot walk more than a step or two from bed to wheelchair, but she is pretty good with that step, and even better with the chair. In short, she gets around. Because we want to support an interest in the outside world, we subscribe to her very own copy of the Detroit Free Press. We also subscribe, at her request, to a second paper. It is the second paper that she reads more diligently. After all, inquiring minds want to know. I take it as a sign that she is failing.

My grandmother talks about dying a lot. No, I take that back. My grandmother jokes about dying a lot. She knows that she has outlived her compatriots in the old Yugoslav community who migrated to Detroit in the early twenties. She knows that ninety-seven percent of the people on her once-extensive Christmas card list are dead. She sees the other two ladies in her room are non-verbal, non-mobile, and largely non-rational, and is scared to death that what they have might be catching. Three years ago, I rushed to Providence Hospital in order to reiterate her wish that no heroic measures be used. Then I sat down with a small cadre of family to wait for the end. She was sure that she was dying. She said so. In fact, she made a most eloquent good-bye speech, folded her arms across her chest and closed her eyes to die. Except, she didn't die. Surprised, and somewhat unnerved by this, she made the same speech again some ten minutes later. It was a good line to go out on. Except that the curtain never dropped. Somebody backstage missed a marvelous cue.

Today, she is very much alive, although I have reason to believe she'd just as soon not be. She is not a whiner, crier, or complainer, although if somebody crosses her, she still has a way of getting her point across. I wouldn't want to leave you with the impression that she is lying there, crying the prayer of the whipped and the weary, "Oh Jesus, won't you please take me?" Things aren't that bad. No pity sought or needed. Still, she'd like to die. She says so … to everybody who comes near. If you were to meet my grandmother this afternoon, she would say something like this: "I talked to St. Peter the other day and asked him if he had any room. And St. Peter said to me, "Agnes, still no vacancy." (Although she substitutes a "w" for the "v," so that it comes out, "no wacancy.") Then she laughs. Her laughter affirms her life, such as it is. It also, I suspect, beats crying.

Which brings us to Cherie DeRose … a leaf in the springtime … fallen (as it were) very much out of season. Her death has touched us deeply, moving us (as such deaths always do) to bewilderment and anger in the midst of tears. Her death seems neither fair nor right. And if you came expecting me to paint a picture in which her death could somehow be prettied up so as to make it appear "fair" or "right," you have come to the wrong artist. For I cannot envision a world in which "fairness" or "rightness" could include her dying.

A very fine lady and life-long Christian came up to me at yesterday's Boutique and said, "If you can say anything that will help me understand why someone like her had to die …" She didn't even finish the sentence. She didn't need to. This lady has been in the church for over fifty years. She knows as many answers as I do. Probably more. She's been a part of moments like this more times than I have. Hers is not a lack of faith. Hers is not an untutored spirit. Hers is not even a personal loss, for (in her words), "I hardly even know the family." Hers is simply the gut-wrenching response that all of us feel when something does not follow "in due season."

Cherie was young: thirty-eight. Cherie was active: in church, school, neighborhood, and community. Cherie was vital: a small package of energy that could light up a room. Cherie was committed: to Ed in a seventeen-year marriage. Cherie was needed: by three daughters (Katee, Lindsay, and Merrill), with one of them likely to need her far deeper and longer than ordinary. Cherie was enjoyed: by a host of preschoolers who resonated with her personality and sang her silly songs. And Cherie was cherished: by no small number of friends who now have a hole in their circle along with fresh reason to question their own invincibility. In talking about "why someone like her had to die," the emphasis is every bit as much on the "someone like her" as it is on the "had to die." All of us have to die, death being one of life's seasons. But not this season, for Cherie's sake … please.

It would not, of course, be my opinion that Cherie DeRose "had" to die. It would not be my opinion that her "season" was somehow penciled in, as having to be "here and now" rather than "there and later." It would not be my opinion that there is anything predetermined or fatalistic about such timings. I do not believe that a close examination of the bookwork of heaven would find the day of her death logged there in advance. There are many who would say, "Her time came. Therefore, there was nothing anybody could do." I would simply ask those people to consider the alternative: "Because there was nothing anybody could do, her time came."

Ironically, the book of Ecclesiastes does not agree with me. When the old sage talks about a season for everything, he clearly sees the seasons as being fixed, with no way of avoiding them. What is, is. And that's how it was meant to be. He sees life as a series of fixed and predetermined events. We meet them at the appointed hour. Everything occurs when it must occur. There is no deviation from plan. It is a variation of the old argument, which suggests: "If the bullet has your name on it, it will find you. If it doesn't, it won't."

There are a lot of people who still believe that way. I talked with one of them in the wake of Cherie's death. Said he, to me, "I guess when your time is up, you have to go … at least that's what the preachers say. "Not all of them," I answered. Then I asked him what he thought. "Well, I'm not very religious," he began. "I just figured that's pretty much what most people believe. When God needs you, God's gonna get you."

I said that I wasn't sure that I saw it the same way. I said that I found it hard to conceive of God needing Cherie more than Katee needed Cherie. I said that I imagined God feeling as much pain as we were feeling about now. And I may have said a couple of other things besides. If so, I forget. But I said them quietly, conversationally, certainly not argumentatively. Long ago I learned to not mess with somebody's belief system at the hour of death. Still, it seemed to me that he liked what I was saying better than what he thought preachers believed. Maybe it was the first time he ever considered that while God graciously **received** Cherie in the wee small hours of last Thursday morning, God didn't necessarily **take** Cherie in the wee small hours of last Thursday morning.

Yesterday morning, a friend of mine who is genuinely concerned for my welfare said, "I don't envy your job, knowing that once more you've got to stand up and look down at all those people, knowing that every one of them has the same unspoken question chiseled upon their lips … the question, 'why?'" And if that is your only question, I must confess that answering it would require a theological autopsy that I am not sufficiently skilled to perform. For I do not know, in the last analysis, why Cherie DeRose died. I do not know why Peter VandenBelt or Roger Jones died. I do not know why Holly Pawl died. I do not know why Craig Kahl died. I do not know why David Ehlers died. Neither do I know why other lovely leaves fall in the all-too-early spring.

But I do know the answer to another question. It is not a "why" question but a "who" question. I know **Who** has gone before us, in his own unseasonable death. I know **Who** will see us through, at the hour of our own. I know **Who** shall receive us unto himself, once our time on earth is done.

David H.C. Reed, now of Madison Avenue Presbyterian

The DeRose family, Ed and Cherie and their daughters.

Church in New York, was a native of Scotland whose faith was stripped to the bare essentials during a stint as a prisoner of war. He writes, " I believe in the Christian gospel, not because it offers the best explanation of human suffering, but because it gives us the One we need to lead us through."

I believe that. And have seen the Healing One at work in this congregation, in the person of those who have reached out and rallied round, who have been there from moment one … people like Mark and Dave and Kris, Sue and Jan, Cindi, Bev, and all the others who came to the fore on November 1, not even thinking about the fact that it was All Saints Day. All of them were short on answers but long on love. None of them knew the right words to say, but all of them stuttered and stammered with true eloquence.

"Cling very close to each other tonight," the young lovers are told in Flower Drum Song. It was a truly memorable lyric. It is also marvelously descriptive of Christians at their best. My friends, hold each other close. Hold each other up. And so fulfill the law of Christ.

November 4, 1990
Nardin Park United Methodist Church
Farmington Hills, Michigan

14

WHO'S GONNA STAY WITH US?

Every leave-taking means that as someone goes, someone else gets left behind. This sermon, while first preached at Nardin Park UMC, was ultimately recast as a Maundy Thursday sermon at Birmingham First UMC in 1999. I then re-preached it, again on Maundy Thursday, in 2005. To the best of my memory, it was the only time I ever re- preached the same sermon in the same church. But in 2005, it was the year of my immanent departure via retirement. And, as such, it was the entire congregation that was feeling left behind.

Scripture: John 14 (selected portions)

Let me script a number of scenarios ... slices of life, really ... the better that you might place yourself within them, or feel yourself inside them.

You are a child. Perhaps an only child. Perhaps one of a number of children. But you are not old enough to be an independent child ... meaning that you are not old enough to stay on your own. Along about 5:00 p.m., you see the first telltale sign. Having seen it before, you know exactly what it means. Your mother takes a shower, does her hair, reaches for the "serious" makeup rather than the "anything to make myself presentable" makeup, even to the point of spraying perfume from the fancy bottle (the one she told your father was much too expensive to wear, but never quite returned for a refund). Or, the sign could include similar preparatory acts on the part of your father. Or even the appearance of the delivery kid from Dominos, impatiently knocking on your front door.

Instantly, you knew. They were going out. And you were staying home. Which, if you were like me, gave birth to all kinds of feelings. And all kinds of questions. Like:

Are you going out?

(And if you wanted to press the guilt button extra hard, you added the word "again" to the end of the question.)

Am I staying home?

Where are you going?

Why can't I go, too?

When are you coming home?

Can I stay up 'til you get here?

Followed by the inevitable:

Who's gonna stay with me?

And wise is the parent who knows that there had better be some answer to questions 1-6, but a very good answer to question 7.

Or you are a mother. An older mother. A very much older mother. A very much older, widowed mother. Who lives in a retirement home ... which is something of a down payment on a nursing home ... which (perish the thought) is something of a down payment on a funeral home. But the retirement home is comfortable. And your son is near. Your only son ... who is married to your only daughter-in-law ... and is the father of your only grandchildren (anywhere on the face of the earth). So how do you feel when the employer of this up-and-coming son ... who thinks every bit as much of him as you do ... tells him that she has created a new vice presidency, just for him. In Rio de Janeiro. For at least three years.

Who's gonna stay with me?

Or you are a couple, new to a town. You look high and low for a church ... the right church ... which (when you find it) you know it by "feel" rather than by "label." And a big part of the "feel" is the preacher ... who (even though you hate to admit it) is the real reason you decided to join. We're talking about the same preacher who asks for a moment of personal privilege on the Sunday after you join, and says, "This is a bittersweet day for me. For I must tell you that, just last Friday, I accepted a call to be the minister of First Church, Fairtown." And among the audible murmurs of surprise from the people around you, you hear the half-formed voice of your subconscious saying:

Who's gonna stay with us?

Or you are a partner in a firm that felt good ... paid good ... did good ... until the day you realized that one of the reasons you were "making out like bandits," is that some of your partners were making out like bandits. Not with guns or masks, but with computers and erasers. Since you weren't in the candy business, you knew that the words "fudge factor" didn't have anything to do with your product line. So, over time, you gathered the right facts ... asked the right questions ... drew the right conclusions ... and stood the right ground. You did so quietly, setting up a decidedly non-showy showdown. But, in the end, nothing happened to your partners. Instead, you and your family were the ones who went from being marginalized to ostracized. And did you not inquire:

Is anybody gonna stay with us?

I could paint half a dozen more pictures ... not of what it means to leave ... but of how it feels to be left. By whomever. For whatever. Whether it be a spouse who goes ... kids who go ... friends who go ... parishioners who go ... even God who goes ("Why hast thou forsaken me?") ... it hurts to be the one who hears the message about the going, but doesn't get to do the going. Even when people die on us (which would seem to be a legitimate reason to go, if ever there was one), there is often an anger that smolders quietly ... for who would dare express it ... an anger that says: "Damn you for leaving me."

Who's gonna stay with us?

•••••

We strive to become self-sufficient and comfortable with our solitude. But few of us ever graduate with advanced degrees in either self-sufficiency or solitude. Which is why we cannot understand Henry David Thoreau, when he acclaimed, that he had but three chairs in his house: "One for solitude, two for company, and three for society." No, it is for us that George Orwell wrote (in his essay, "Pleasure Spots"):

The lights must never go out

The music must always play

Lest we should see where we are,

Alone in a haunted wood.

You know where this is going, don't you? Of course, you do. That's why I like preaching to you. Because, even in the dark, lights come on faster in your heads than almost anywhere else. Which means that you're way ahead of me, here. You've already figured out that I'm taking you downtown (to old Jerusalem) and upstairs (to that borrowed second-story dining room). And don't you wish you knew how they managed to find a caterer ... on short notice ... at Passover ... in a strange city. But I digress. Back to the table.

Where he said to his friends, "I'm going away, to a place where you can't go. At least not yet." When suddenly it hit them ... what it all meant ... all this talk about how "the Son of Man must suffer and die." To which Peter had (earlier) said: "Lord, this will never happen to you ... at least not while I'm around." But now it was going to happen to him, in spite of the fact that Peter was around.

What it all boiled down to ... up there ... for them ... was that Jesus was going to die his way out of their lives. And, at that point, they couldn't have cared less about the reason, the purpose, or any potential benefit that might be derived from his passing. Whatever else the disciples may have said in the Upper Room, not one of them voiced an opinion on the Atonement ... or stood up on a chair to demonstrate that he had memorized John 3:16.

No, they were scared stiff. They were frightened. "Let not your hearts be troubled," he said ... for which the proper translation is: "Let not your hearts tremble and shake." Which he wouldn't have said if their hearts weren't ... trembling and shaking, that is.

So what came out of their mouths in the midst of it all? If we believe John 14, they said a couple of quotable things like:

> Thomas: "We don't know the way. How can we know the way?"

> Philip: "Just show us the Father, and we shall be satisfied."

But I think they said some less quotable things that weren't written down. Like:

Are you going out?

Are we staying home?

Where are you going?

Why can't we go, too?

How long before you'll be back?

Can we stay in Bartholomew's room until you get here?

Followed by the inevitable:

Who's gonna stay with us?

How do I know that? Not because I was there. But because I've been there. And because Jesus addressed that question, head on. "I will not leave you desolate," he said. Which has also been translated: "I will not leave you comfortless." But the very best translation reads: "I will not leave you orphaned." Which is when he tells them that the Spirit will come. And it does. To them. To us. At all kinds of times. And at all kinds of places. But always to supper.

When I was a little boy, I went with my mother to church one Maundy Thursday. We sat near the back ... in the candlelight. Which meant the big, old church was lovely. But very dark. And Holy Communion in that church was at the rail ... by rows. One row at a time. But Holy Communion was not for little boys. At least not at that time. So when the usher came to call my row, he somehow indicated I should stay. Which I did. Alone. It wasn't my mother's fault. She didn't know the "drill" any better than I did. But there I was, the sole remaining occupant of my pew. And when the row behind me followed, I felt even more alone. Because my row hadn't come back yet, don't you see? I didn't know what any of this was about ... and why everyone else had gone. And I cried. Because nobody stayed with me.

But now I am a bigger boy ... one who's not only been to church, but been to supper. Where I've heard the Lord. And felt the Spirit. And every day ... and most nights ... that's been enough. Yes, that's been enough.

April 1, 1999, Maundy Thursday
First United Methodist Church
Birmingham, Michigan

15

VISIONS OF WRIGLEY FIELD ON A SATURDAY AFTERNOON

As a lifelong baseball fan (sometimes called a fanatic) this is my favorite sermon title. Judging from the number of reprints that flew off the rack and resurfaced nationwide once I preached this, it remains one of my best-read sermons ever. And yes, I really have been to Wrigley Field ... albeit on a Monday, not a Saturday.

Scripture: II Corinthians 4:16-5:5

For the life of me (or for the life of him), I don't know what happened to Robert Fulghum. Several years ago, he burst on the scene with a book of homespun essays entitled, *All I Really Need to Know I Learned in Kindergarten*. It was good stuff. It was also popular stuff. Books flew off the shelves so fast he wrote six more. The best one (for my money, anyway) was entitled, *From Beginning to End: The Rituals of Our Lives*.

185

Turn with me (in your imagination, anyway) to page 28 where you will find a most unusual picture. It shows a man sitting in a beach chair amidst the tombstones of a cemetery. We later learn that the man owns the property on which he sits. More to the point, he is sitting on his own grave. Not because his death is imminent … he's in pretty good shape, actually. And not because he was in a morbid state of mind when the picture was taken. To the contrary, he claims it was one of the most affirmative afternoons in his life.

I do not own a grave. But if I had one, I doubt I'd visit it … let alone sit upon it. Still, it's worthy of contemplation. Were I going to sit for an afternoon over the place I was going to lay for eternity, what kind of chair might I use? Beach chair? Deck chair? Lawn chair? La-Z-Boy chair? I think I'd prefer a recliner, given that I could both kick back and look up … which, as postures go, would be both physically correct and theologically appropriate.

Not that I dwell on such things, mind you. My hope is that, like Robert Frost's traveler "stopping in the woods on a snowy evening," I really do have miles to go before I sleep. But even the nimble-footed can't dodge death. And even though I ran a trio of 10K races in my mid-fifties, nobody ever called me nimble of foot. "Plodding" would be a better word to describe my pace and gait now. So, as with many of you, my mind occasionally turns to the time I have left … and to what follows after what's left is gone. This could lead to a doctrinal sermon on the prospect of heaven or a speculative sermon on the furniture of heaven. But, concerning the "prospect," Paul says, "It's a certainty." And concerning the "furniture," Paul says, "It's a mystery." And who am I to one-up Paul? I am confident that God has prepared something … that God's "something" will be a very good thing … and that I won't know anything more until such time as God's "good thing" becomes my thing.

But that has never stopped the guesswork, either from scholars or from simpletons. Dante pictured heaven as a seven-story pyramid, while Kinsella pictured heaven as a baseball field in Iowa. If those are my only two choices, I'll go with the baseball field in Iowa. Which explains why I love the full-page picture from Baseball Weekly, featuring a long-suffering Cub fan saying: "If heaven is anything like Wrigley Field on a Saturday afternoon, I am not afraid to die." Which calls to mind that marvelous story about the fellow who died and fried down below for several years. Then, one day, he felt a coolish breeze or two, followed by hints of a frost, followed by the actual formation of ice crystals in the air. All of which led him to turn to his friend in chilled amazement and say, "I guess the Cubs just won the pennant."

As for me, I find myself caring less and less about where I go, and more and more about whom I go to. I suppose you could fashion an entire theology around that distinction. And the issue is so serious that the only way we can comfortably talk about it is with humor.

> A three-year-old little girl has a cat.
> Cat dies, flattened like a pancake
>   under the wheels of a semi.
> Little girl to mommy, "Where is Fluffy now?"
> Mommy to little girl, "Fluffy is with God, my dear."

Little girl (claiming the last word),
"Don't be silly, Mommy. What would
God want with a squished old cat?"

One hopes that mommy trusts the imagination of God enough to say, "Plenty."

A clergy journal tells me that my Presbyterian colleague, Morgan Roberts, has published a collection of sermons entitled, *Are There Horses in Heaven*? Not having read the book, I don't know Morgan's answer. But he would never have fashioned such a title unless he had a personal investment in the outcome. As to what that may be, only Morgan can say. I don't know whether Morgan wants horses in heaven so he can ride 'em, breed 'em, or bet 'em. I do know that C.S. Lewis expects to have sex in heaven (that is if God is even half as good as Lewis thinks He is).

But none of us knows, do we? At least we don't know for sure. That's because we are on the wrong side of a "frosty glass," says Paul ... the other side being the "face-to-face" side. If only we could see clearer, we could feel better. About dying, that is. Although some claim to have seen more than enough to convince them. They tell stories of how they almost died but didn't. Instead, they came back. But all they could describe was a tunnel, a powerful light, and a reception of incredible kindness. Still, it made believers out of those who weren't. And it buttressed the confidence of those who were.

Seen or unseen, something of a heavenly vision gave Paul his confidence, allowing him to say to the Corinthians, "Though our outer nature be wasting away, our inner nature is being renewed, day by day." Following which, he continues, "For this slight momentary affliction ..."

> Can you believe what Paul is saying?
> Cancer, a slight momentary affliction?
> Rheumatoid arthritis, a slight momentary affliction?
> Alzheimer's, a slight momentary affliction?
> MS ... ALS ... TB ... HIV ...
> slight momentary afflictions?

An old friend called me from Ohio on Friday. I hadn't talked to him in years. The purpose of his call was to tell me about twelve tumors ... all of them malignant ... ten of them in his brain and two of them in his lung. I did not suggest that he think of them as "slight momentary afflictions."

But we need to give Paul his due. At least we need to let him finish his sentence. "For this slight momentary affliction is preparing us for an eternal weight of glory, beyond all comparison. Because we do not look to the things that are seen, but to the things that are unseen." For it is in the "unseen things," Paul says, that we find clues to our destiny.

But concerning "the things that are unseen," are we forced to walk by faith alone? Or is it possible (as we draw closer and closer to them) that we can also walk by sight? From this point on, the burden of my sermon will be to convince you ... or at least suggest to you ... that we walk by sight. For I would suggest that scales do fall from our eyes at the hour of our dying ... perhaps even before ... so that we can glimpse some of the things that are eternal, not just at the hour of our clinical death, but (in many cases) hours ... even days ... before our clinical death.

In a lovely little book entitled *A Year to Live,* Stephen Levine writes:

> Death, like birth, is not so much an emergency as an emergence. Those who know the process directly do not speak of death as a single moment (before which you are alive and after which you are not), so much as a point where holding onto life transforms itself as a letting go into death.

All I know is that some years ago it struck me that very few people die frightened. Very few people die agitated. People seem to die peacefully. Even those who were previously afraid and distressed, die calm. Having been where people die, I can tell you that it is seldom, if ever, horrible. I can also tell you that it occasionally borders on the beautiful. Not that I am always there at the last minute. That's because a disproportionately high number of people die without anybody in the room. I almost said that a disproportionately high number of people die alone. But that would be wrong. I don't mean "alone." I mean "without anybody in the room." It's a distinction to which I will return in a couple of minutes.

Why is there so little fear at the hour of death? Could it be narcotics, administered by physicians? Perhaps. Could it be narcotics, self-generated by the brain? Perhaps. But let me suggest another possibility. Let me suggest that people are "transitioned" from death to life by spiritual presences that include everything from God himself to that "incredible cloud of witnesses," which is a biblical euphemism for what the church has commonly called "the communion of saints" … or who my late North Carolina colleague, Carlyle Marney, loved to call "the balcony people."

It was a doctor in an intensive care unit who first suggested this to me. We were talking about my parishioner … his patient … who was still capable of sight, speech and conscious awareness of his environment. But he preferred remaining silent, even though his eyes often seemed to be following something other than us. After watching this for a while, the physician remarked, "Would you keep your eyes open to look at these walls, these tubes, these machines?" And when I doubted that I would, the doctor concluded, "I think the pictures Harry sees in his head are a whole lot prettier than the pictures Harry sees when he opens his eyes."

But are the "pretty pictures" self-created or sent? Or could they be both? Some years back, I conducted a memorial service for a man my age. He was a gifted teacher and an able administrator. Kids loved him. Adults loved him. He was a tough, warm, friend-making, fun-loving kind of guy. He was also, insofar as I knew, utterly un-churched. Cancer got him. Got him quick. But just before he died, he told his wife about the most vivid dream he had ever had in his life. He was sailing on an ocean. Alone. Toward a beautiful sunset. Suddenly he sailed toward a rock, upon which was seated a man. The man was well dressed and clean-shaven. Smiling, the man beckoned. The man on the rock was his father. And, in a matter of hours, my friend joined his daddy in death.

Sometimes it's less a dream and more a vision. I have had dying people describe faces I couldn't see ... but they could. And I have heard dying people talk to folks I couldn't hear ... but they could. I once asked a member of my choir, who was as alert in dying as most of us are in living: "Glenn, do you see anybody you know ... people who have gone ... but who may now be coming to be with you?" And although he couldn't talk, the smile on his face, coupled with the strength in the squeeze of his hand, told me all I wanted to know.

Not so long ago, one of my dearest friends died following a multi-year battle with malignancy. She died at home, as was her wish. In the last hour of her life, I baptized her grandchild (newly arrived from California) in her bedroom. She held onto consciousness long enough to tell Kris where to find the Waterford bowl on her sideboard. Then she held the baby. When I was finished, she let go. And when the end came, her husband said, "She had a calling. She did not go by herself. It was the most beautiful thing I ever saw."

Three nights previous, after making it clear to the people at Providence Hospital that she was leaving, come hell or high water, she whispered to me, "I'm going home." To which I said: "That's right, Jan. Frank's coming to take you in the morning." To which she said, "No, you don't understand. I'm going home." To which I added, "Say hi to our son."

Earlier, I said that most people die with no one in the room. They die when you and I step out for coffee. They die when we slip home to shower. They die when the doctor forces us to get some sleep. I think they die without us because they are afraid for us … not for themselves. Which is why the best gift we can give a dying loved one is permission to go. I recently buried a man who hung on … hung on … and hung on some more, defying everybody's expectations. Then, late on a Sunday, everyone left to go to supper. Except for his grandson, who quietly said, "Go see Grandma, big guy." And in a matter of minutes, "big guy"

The iconic ivy-covered outfield wall at Wrigley Field awaits any player attempting to thwart a homerun hit.

did. But, you see, if I am right about being transitioned ... and I think I am ... it doesn't matter if anybody is in the room. Because nobody dies alone.

In closing, let me leave you with this. From time to time, I am invited to preach in a distant city, necessitating a flight of some duration. Invariably, someone on the destination end will offer to meet me at the airport. I always decline the offer. Not because I am anti-social. But because I am considerate. I know that people lead busy lives and have other needs. Besides, I'm a big boy. I can get on a plane. I can get off a plane. I can grab my bag. I can hail a cab. I can get wherever it is I need to be, whenever I need to be there. I am well schooled in such things.

Still, there is often a change of heart when I reach my destination. The plane descends and taxies across the tarmac. Finally, it butts its nose against the body of the building, and everything shuts down. At the very same moment, everybody stands up. Don't ask me why we do that ... stand up together, I mean. Those of us in row 27 aren't going anywhere. But we stand up anyway. Collectively, we reach for our overhead luggage. Slowly, we inch our way down the center aisle. Upon reaching the front of the aircraft, we see the captain and one of the flight attendants. Both are smiling. Speaking with one voice, they express hope that we enjoyed our flight. We tell them we did (whether we mean it or not). Then we deplane.

Four steps to the left get us out of the aircraft and into the jet-way. The jet-way is that rolling corridor that has been wheeled into place to link the airplane to the building (resembling a Habitrail for humans). Once in the jet-way, we turn right. It's the only way we're going to get to the terminal. Prior to 9/11, it was after making the right turn that we could see the faces coming into view. What faces? The faces waiting for deplaning passengers. Craning their necks, they are waiting for us to walk into view. There are wives waiting for husbands, and husbands waiting for wives. There are little kids perched on somebody's shoulders, looking for a grandparent. And there are people with white hair and bifocals waiting for grandchildren. Along with neighbors waiting for neighbors ... friends waiting for friends ... and lovers waiting for lovers (who will clog the works by passionately embracing in the midst of the flow). And there are others who are not even certain who they are waiting for. They are the ones holding those hand-lettered signs.

As I start toward those faces, I never look up. I know I won't recognize anybody. I told my friends not to bother meeting me. After all, I'm a big boy and can take of myself. Which is true. But with each passing step, I find myself scanning the crowd ... searching the faces ... in the hope that just one of them (just one of them) will be waiting there for me.

•••••

I don't know about you, but the older I get, the less interest I have in eternal life ... if, by eternal life, you mean endless extension (going on, and on, and on, etc.). But if you mean blessed reunion, then you've captured my interest. Because having lived this long, I have lost far too many to want it any other way.

As for heaven's landscape, I'll wait for the surprise. Not without my own fantasies, given that we all entertain them. You want pearly gates and golden streets? Be my guest. You want lush golf courses and unrestricted tee times? Be my guest. I'll be satisfied with passing through the turnstile, emerging through the portal, and gazing upon a diamond that is green, complete with bases that are white, on a day that is sunny ... rejoicing that my ticket has already been paid for ... and the crowd, much bigger than I expected.

July 2007
Northville United Methodist Church
Northville, Michigan

Notes: Robert Fulghum's gravesite reflections appear in his book, *From Beginning to End: The Rituals of Our Lives*, published by Villard Books, A Division of Random House, in 1995. At the time of this printing, Fulghum spends his time between Moab, Utah and the Greek island of Crete.

16

HEAVEN IN A CORNFIELD

Continuing with the theme of my last two sermons (namely, what happens when we go?), I offer another ... this one inspired by the film Field of Dreams. Could it be that the game of baseball really does inspire theological reflection? I'd be more than willing to join the late Bart Giamatti in making that argument.

Scriptures: Matthew 5:21-26, Revelation 21 (selected verses)

It is rare when people remember their dreams. And it is "rarer still" when they reveal them. But Dave Breedlove remembered and revealed one of his the other day. And if I am recalling it accurately, it went something like this:

I dreamed (Dave said) that Dale Parker died and went to heaven. Upon checking his record at the gate, St. Peter said, "I am sorry, Dale, but I have found a few blemishes on your otherwise pristine page, meaning that you are going to have to do a little bit of penance before you can stay." Whereupon St. Peter proceeded to chain Dale at the ankle to one of the meanest, nastiest and ugliest women he had ever seen.

Dale took all of this in stride, figuring that a few months of penance would be a pittance, compared to the eternity of bliss that would surely follow. And Dale was fine with this until he saw his preacher walking along, similarly chained at the ankle, to Julia Roberts. Seething with resentment, Dale worked his way back to St. Peter who was tending the gate. "I don't get it," Dale shouted. "Here I am sentenced to perform what you call 'a little bit of penance,' and I end up chained to the meanest, nastiest and ugliest woman I have ever seen. And there goes Ritter, chained at his ankle to Julia Roberts." To which St. Peter replied: "Dale, settle down. There is something you don't understand. Ritter is Julia's penance."

I tell that story with a definite purpose in mind. Not to debate the relative fitness of Dale Parker and myself for heaven. Not to create speculation about Dave Breedlove's dream life. And certainly not to get a cheap laugh from the likes of you. Trust me. I have bigger fish to fry.

I also tell that story to illustrate a great truth about humor. Most of us joke about things that confuse us, or give us cause for anxiety. Humor is one of the best ways we have of relieving anxiety. I am convinced that anxiety lies behind the many jokes we tell about sex. And I am similarly convinced that anxiety lies behind the many jokes we tell about death. In a strange way, Dave's dream is a joke about both.

But in reflecting upon this, I got to thinking of all the jokes about someone who died and approached St. Peter. There must be hundreds of them. Which must mean we are pretty anxious about death and whatever follows. Questions abound.

Where will we go?

When will we get there?

What will we do there?

Who will we see there?

Will we meet our loved ones there?

Will there be any judgment there?

Will there be any justice there?

Will there be any fulfillment there ...

... especially for those who have died too soon ...

... died too sinful ...

... or died too separated?

Such questions give rise to humor. They also give rise to reverie, along with philosophy and theology. They have been around a long time. And they have never been fully answered. The Apostle Paul fingered the problem when he said: "Hey friends ... it's a mystery. We shall not all sleep; we shall all be changed." Then Paul spent forty-four verses of the fifteenth chapter of First Corinthians trying to explain the very thing he called "a mystery." Paul should have left well enough alone. His attempt is about as Greek as the language in which he wrote it.

With that in mind, cut away with me to a quiet, midsummer's night in an Iowa cornfield. Darkness is settling. Crickets are chirping. Gentle breezes are rippling the tassels of corn, richly buttered by the moonlight. A young man named Ray Kinsella is trudging from field to farmhouse when he hears the voice ... a whisper really ... sounding something like God with laryngitis or an old baseball announcer. The voice is saying (in words barely audible): "If you build it, he will come." Ray shrugs off the voice and heads for the house. But later that night he hears it again, waking him from a sound sleep. The next day he hears the voice a third time: "If you build it, he will come."

And lest there be any question about their meaning, the words are accompanied by a vision. There is little doubt in Ray's mind that the "it" he is to build is a baseball field ... complete with bleachers and bases, fences and foul lines, scoreboards and floodlights, the whole nine yards. And the "he" who will come is Joe Jackson ... Shoeless Joe Jackson ... who, in the opinion of Ty Cobb, was the greatest left fielder ever to play the game.

Shoeless Joe never learned to read and write, but he created legends with his bat and glove. A famous sportswriter once wrote that Joe Jackson's glove was the place where triples went to die. Shoeless Joe played a dozen years in the big leagues, but the ending of his career was not of his choosing. He was the left fielder for the Chicago White Sox when they won the American League pennant in 1919. They were subsequently accused of "throwing" the World Series to the Cincinnati Reds. For their alleged involvement with gamblers, the team was dubbed the "Black Sox," and eight players were suspended from baseball for life. The most notable of these was Shoeless Joe Jackson. It was that suspension that caused one disbelieving little boy to utter the immortal line, "Say it ain't so, Joe." But all Joe said in response was: "It's so." And evidently, it was.

Ray Kinsella was raised on Joe Jackson stories by his father, Johnny Kinsella, who once lived in a rooming house across the street from Comiskey Park. He also caught a few games of Class B ball in his all-too-brief career. Ray's daddy went to his grave believing that Joe Jackson was innocent ... that he was framed ... and that the whole thing was just another example of the powerful oppressing the poor. For, in those days, baseball players were neither well paid nor well treated. They were virtual pawns of a management system that abused and underpaid them.

Ray's father was quick to point out that Joe Jackson hit .375 against the Reds in the 1919 Series. In addition, he played errorless ball and banged out 12 hits. To Ray's dad, that didn't sound like the record of a man trying to "throw" a game. But not enough other people bought that logic. After the 1920 season, when Shoeless Joe hit .382, he was never allowed to play in the "bigs" again. He drifted from one semi-pro league to another, usually playing under an assumed name. If honor and glory ever do come his way, he won't be around to take a bow ... given that he died (in relative obscurity) in 1951.

But Ray Kinsella ... trusting the voice and obeying the vision ... is certain that Shoeless Joe will come to his field, once he builds it. Concerning that vision, Ray says, "Occasionally the time and place are right, when all the cosmic tumblers click into place, and the universe opens up for a few seconds ... or a few hours ... and shows you what is possible."

What a marvelous line. What he's saying is that every now and then things just seem to click and the heavens open, giving a glimpse of how it is all going to work out.

Now if you are about to say, "Come on, Ritter, that's the dumbest thing I ever heard," remember that Martin Luther King said the same thing in his Memphis speech the night before he died. He was talking about the Civil Rights Movement. And he was saying that the movement would go on, even though he would not get to go on with it. He said he had been to the mountain ... all the way to the top ... and that he had been privileged to look over to the other side. And what he glimpsed convinced him that everything was going to be all right.

Moments ago, we read the same thing in the twenty-first chapter of Revelation. Revelation is a strange book ... more allegory than history. It is told as a grand vision. And the man to whom the vision comes is someone named John. We think he was an exiled bishop of the early Christian church in Asia Minor. He appears to have been imprisoned ... being held on a Mediterranean island named Patmos ... during a period when Christians were being zealously persecuted by Rome.

The language of the book is called the language of Apocalypse, which means that it is concerned with someone's vision of how things are going to end up. And in chapter 21, John says that he was, for a moment, transported into heaven in order to receive just such a vision. I don't have the faintest idea what that means … or how that happened. Was it a dream? An ecstatic experience? A photographic revelation? A sudden blip on the radar screen of consciousness? Was John fast-forwarded in time (by God) in order to allow him to drink in the future, before being rewound into ordinary time? Was John's vision an answer to prayer? A projection of the imagination? The result of a hallucinogenic? Darned if I know. But, then, I don't claim to know how Martin Luther King glimpsed the Promised Land either. But when he talked about it, I listened. And I found I was leaning forward as I listened. So maybe Ray Kinsella has it figured out as well as anybody. Perhaps there are times when all the cosmic tumblers do click into place, and the universe opens up for a few seconds, giving a glimpse of what is possible.

In the twenty-first chapter of Revelation, it is not a ballpark that John sees, but an entire city. The city is like a virgin bride being presented to her husband. New Jerusalem is the city's name. Old Jerusalem was to have been the perfect city. But at the time of John's vision, Old Jerusalem is under siege … sacked and burning.

The new city will be a place of peace and harmony. That's what John says. God himself will be there. It will be like the Garden of Eden all over again. Things will be like they were before the Fall … before we messed things up. Once again, God will walk through the city in the cool of the evening.

It will be a city without violence … without pain … without tears. God will be like a mother comforting her children, wiping every last tear from their eyes. There shall be no more death in the city … meaning that the thing we fear more than any other will be relegated to the scrap heap that we call "former things."

And it will be a city without churches. There will be no temple there. To my friend who says he doesn't want to go to heaven if it is going to be like a boring church service, this will be good news indeed. There won't be any churches, temples, synagogues, cathedrals, or wayside chapels, says John. That's because God will be right there with us. Therefore, we will have no need for special places, set apart for the purpose of meeting him.

There will be neither sun nor moon in the city. The dazzling brightness of God's glory … and the "lamp" that we call Jesus Christ … will give us all the light we need.

And, most significantly, all the nations will be there. Even the pagan nations. Which means that the barriers we build to separate us, one from another, will have come down. It will be a city without walls or other visible lines of demarcation. And good will triumph in the city because no one will be there who is unclean, loathsome or false. And speaking as one who is occasionally unclean, loathsome and false, I trust that the absence of such folk from heaven will have more to do with the fact that God is cleaning us all up, rather than kicking us all out.

And that's John's version of how it all comes out. If that seems archaic and fanciful to you, let me return you (one more time) to Ray Kinsella's farm in Iowa … where Ray hears the voice, builds the park, and Shoeless Joe Jackson comes. Yes, he really comes. But not everybody can see him. Half the town thinks Ray is crazy … plowing up two and a half acres of perfectly good corn to build a ball diamond. It gives you an idea of how Noah's neighbors must have treated him. But Ray's wife never wavers. Neither does Ray's daughter. For they seem to know that some voices need to be heard and heeded. And they can see the ball players, too.

For Shoeless Joe brings his friends with him. His seven suspended teammates from the Black Sox come and play. As do others. But the Black Sox are the "home team" at this diamond. Every night, when the lights come on, the players walk onto the field. They come out of the corn, which rims the outfield. When the game ends, they disappear into the corn from whence they came. Ballplayers just kind of come and go … to and from the corn. And the corn, of course, is death. But the corn never seems like such a terrible place. It's just the corn. That's all it is. Dying is nothing more than walking into it. And whatever follows dying is nothing more than walking out of it. It is remarkably unfrightening.

I've always had a strange fantasy about dying. I don't know where it comes from. But I figure that death will be like walking into a woods I have walked into hundreds of times before. Only, this time, I won't come out … at least not by the way I went in. Then somebody introduced me to that marvelous line about Enoch. It was said that Enoch was a man who walked with God. Then one day God and Enoch walked further than they had ever walked before … and kept on walking.

But if the corn is Kinsella's symbol for death, then the baseball diamond is Kinsella's symbol for heaven. The ballpark is his Apocalypse … his vision … his glimpse of how it all turns out. At one point, Shoeless Joe turns to Ray and says, "Is this heaven?" To which Ray says, "No, it's Iowa." But the longer we watch the movie, the less certain we are as to which is which.

There are some marvelous subplots that keep the story moving. One night Ray hears the voice a second time, and it says, "Ease his pain." Six months of research later, he realizes that the "pain" he is supposed to "ease" belongs to a once-famous author, now living in seclusion on the east coast. In the book, the author is J.D. Salinger. In the movie, it is Terrance Mann (played brilliantly by James Earl Jones). Ray realizes that the author's pain has something to do with baseball and that no healing will take place apart from baseball.

Then, while author and farmer are watching a baseball game at Fenway Park, a third message comes during the fourth inning. This message encourages them to "go the distance." They become convinced that "going the distance" means setting off for Chisholm, Minnesota in order to find Moonlight Graham (who once played half an inning for the New York Giants in 1909 and never got a chance to bat).

Sooner or later, everybody makes it back to Iowa and appears at the ballpark (which may or may not be heaven). And the games constitute a wonderful vision of what the end is going to be like. The Black Sox are playing again (as the home team, no less). The horrible past has been wiped out. The suspensions have been served. The scandal has been forgiven ... forgotten ... vindicated. The slate is clean. Moonlight Graham, who only got to play half an inning in the field in 1909 ... and who never came to bat ... gets to play a whole game now.

What does it all mean? I think this is what it means. As concerns the great game of life, I think that those who played it once ... and who played it wrong ... may get a fresh chance to play it over. Moreover, I think that those who never got much of a chance to play at all ... especially those who were taken by death before they could get a bat in their hands (in order to see what they could do) ... get a chance to play at last. For I think heaven is going to represent a second chance for those who blew the first one, and a fresh chance for those who never got one. That's what I think it means.

But there is one thing more. There is something else in the vision ... something having to do with reconciliation. In the movie, we are given the impression that Ray Kinsella's father not only died young but died estranged from his son. So it becomes inevitable that this ballpark in the cornfield is going to be the scene of some "coming together" of father and son. That's because such reconciliations are as necessary as they are desirable. In our other text ... the one from the Sermon on the Mount ... Jesus said that if there is someone with whom you need to make it right, leave your gift on the way to the altar ... go find that person ... make it right ... and then approach the altar together. And if Jesus really meant that ... assuming that he wasn't talking just to hear himself talk ... I suppose it is also possible that none of us are going to enjoy the fruits of heaven until we complete the same requirement.

At any rate, the moviegoer knows that *Field of Dreams* cannot end before one more figure appears in uniform ... namely, an obscure Class B catcher named Johnny Kinsella. So, one day, as the game breaks up (and the players begin to drift toward the corn), father and son meet at last. They talk a little baseball. Then slowly, and with some hesitation, they begin a game of catch. And that's the third part of the vision. Not only are past wrongs going to be forgiven and missed opportunities going to be granted, but those who are separated from us now are going to be one with us then.

•••••

Some years ago, from this very pulpit, I preached a pair of sermons based on that wonderful Hebrew concept known as "The Blessing." In them, I talked extensively about my father. If you were present then, you know that he died a long time ago ... 31 years this week, and two months after the birth of his first-ever grandchild (who was my firstborn son).

And if you were listening carefully, you know that my father died feeling that his life had been largely unfulfilled. But, then, I suppose my son felt the same way when he died 27 years after his grandfather ... the grandfather who barely knew him when.

But my father and my son were very much alike in another way. Each loved the game of baseball. Each understood the ballet of baseball. Each devoured the statistics of baseball. Each debated the subtleties of baseball. And it was around the subject of baseball that I was able to draw close to each ... especially at times when other avenues were closed or unavailable. My son managed a team (somewhat successfully) in a rotisserie baseball league. And my father was fond of saying that he would have given his right arm to be able to play the game well.

Therefore, if Kinsella's vision even remotely resembles God's plan, I trust that they have found each other ... and that the sound of horsehide meeting leather, even now, punctuates the sweetness of their coming together. But just in case they haven't, I trust that at least one of you will remember to slip a baseball into my casket when I die.

August 9, 1998
First United Methodist Church
Birmingham, Michigan

Note: *Portions of this sermon were originally preached (under the same title) in 1987. At that time, I acknowledged a debt to Mark Trotter for his treatment of a similar theme. Mark once preached in San Diego where his beloved Padres were making a serious run toward a divisional championship and (Mark hoped) much more. As one who was then suffering through a fifth consecutive losing season with the Detroit Tigers, I wished Mark and the Padres well (beneath a veil of thinly-disguised envy).*

17

ON ROTTING IN HELL

Some of you, after reading this title, may decide to skip the next several pages. Be my guest. But you will be missing a fascinating discussion. Don't be put off by the fact that this sermon was first written in 1989. The same issue surfaces repeatedly, given that there are many who derive great visceral pleasure in someone rotting, burning, or otherwise languishing in hell.

Romans 12:9-21; Portions of Psalm 109

Tomorrow night, on prime-time television, one-time Charlie's Angel, Jaclyn Smith, is going to "settle the score" with the man who raped her twenty years ago. I don't know that for a fact. In fact, I'm virtually certain it's fiction. "Settle the Score" is a movie. A made for TV movie. Jaclyn Smith is an actress playing a role in that movie. Her alleged vendetta has been promoted on radio spots for the last several days, complete with the grunts and groans of the rape scene twenty years ago and the teeth-clenching of Ms. Smith announcing: "I'm going to kill him."

This bloody business will take place during the same time frame as "Monday Night Football," illustrating (once again) television's primary contention that the best way to lure viewers from one kind of violence is to give them a different kind of violence, albeit with a seamy slice of sex thrown in for good measure.

I don't even know whether Jaclyn Smith is going to go through with it. I doubt that I'll try to find out. I trust that one of you will call me on Tuesday morning with the news. My only reason for bringing it up this morning is that we have been talking about vengeance, you and I. It is rooted in our nature. We saw that last week. Retaliation is as ancient as scripture and as American as apple pie.

I'll get you for that.

I'll get you for that if it's the last thing I do.

I'll get you for that if it kills me.

We've said it. We've done it. And we've cheered the saying and doing of it by others. Rabbi Harold Kushner has written a new book. Entitled, *Who Needs God*, it is hot off the press. The good rabbi is probably on his way to another bestseller. In an early chapter, I found this personal testimony to the raw appeal of revenge:

> Consider my problem with Clint Eastwood. I have seen only one of his "Dirty Harry" movies, but I

remember it clearly. I've never responded to a movie the way I did to that one, with as strong a sense of divergence between my mind and my gut. Throughout the movie, my mind kept saying: "Why am I watching this? This is cheap, manipulative trash." But at the gut level, my emotional reaction was: "Yeah, go get 'em! Get out the Magnum and blast 'em away. Don't let those punks get away with it." Intellectually, I found it shallow. Emotionally, I found it compelling and satisfying.

The point is not that Rabbi Kushner is a bad person or that the rest of us are any better or worse by comparison. The point is that there is something instinctive in each of us that reacts with a surge of anger to the idea of unpunished villainy. We hate the thought that somewhere, somehow, someone might be getting away with something. Even worse is the thought that the un-avenged perpetrator might actually prosper. Rabbi Kushner, who hit the lecture trail following the publication of his book, *When Bad Things Happen to Good People,* said that the one question he was asked more frequently than any other was the question: "When are you going to write a book about the problem of good things happening to bad people?"

Against such people, we cry out for vengeance. But vengeance is denied us. It is not one of our options. That's one of the things we discovered last week in our probing of the twelfth chapter of Romans. Paul said, in language that couldn't be any plainer, "Do not seek to revenge yourselves on others." Then, cementing his point in the antiquity of ancient Hebrew law, he quoted Deuteronomy 32:35, to wit: "Vengeance belongs to me; I will repay, says the Lord."

What does that mean? We said that it clearly meant that if there is to be any vengeance enacted, it is God's prerogative alone to execute it. But Paul never intended that we enlist God's aid in the retaliatory process. Yet that is precisely what people have done for centuries. They have abused the scriptures. They have said, "All right, God! If revenge is denied to me, you do it for me. Vindicate me, O Lord, against my enemy. Do to him what I would like to do to him, but shouldn't … or can't."

Then I closed last Sunday's sermon with a story. It concerns a young lady who was victimized by "date rape," meaning that she not only knew and trusted her attacker but (prior to the attack) had willingly spent the evening in his company. A child was conceived as a result of that aggression, a child that she carried, bore, and has worked untiringly to feed and clothe.

It has been suggested that the child's father might be willing to shoulder part of the financial burden. He certainly has an obligation to do so. But she wants no part of his money. That's because she wants no part of him. What she does want is to outlive him so she can have the satisfaction of knowing, before she dies, that he is rotting in hell.

That's what she said! She not only believes it, she derives much satisfaction from it. One detects a hint of smugness not unlike that evidenced by Bea Arthur who, in those episodes of the old "Maude" sitcom, would put her husband in his place with the ultimate comeback, "God'll get you for that, Walter."

Now, whether you know it or not, both Maude (who is fictional) and my struggling young mother (who is very real) stand squarely in a biblical tradition that is older than Jesus, older than Paul, and probably as old as the origins of the Old Testament. The desire to enlist God as one's own private playground bully, enforcer or hit man, is evident throughout scripture. But it is especially virulent in the psalms. In fact, there is an entire category of psalms, known as "imprecatory psalms," wherein the writer appeals directly to God in the hope that God will redress some grievance that the writer has with an enemy or a group of enemies. There are several psalms, sufficiently slanted in this manner, so as to be properly called "imprecatory" in nature. But no psalm is more flagrant in its plea for divine retaliation than Psalm 109. As historian Walter Brueggemann points out, Psalm 109 is not the sort of thing one expects to find in the more "edifying" parts of the Bible. We read it a moment ago. But let me roll a bit of its vindictive vitriol back over you, the better that you may feel the weight of its anger and its pain:

Be not silent, O God of my praise!
For wicked and deceitful mouths are open against me.
Speaking against me with lying tongues.
They beset me with words of hate.
And attack me without cause.

Appoint a wicked man against him;
Let an accuser bring him to trial.
When he is tried, let him come forth guilty;
Let his prayer be counted as sin!

May his days be few;

May another seize his goods!
May his children be fatherless,
And his wife a widow!
May his children wander about and beg;
May they be driven out of the ruins they inhabit!
May creditors seize all that he has;
May strangers plunder the fruits of his toil!

Let there be none to extend kindness to him,
Nor any to pity his fatherless children!

May his posterity be cut off;
May his name be blotted out by the second generation.

What do we have here? What we have, suggests Brueggemann, is "a raw, undisciplined song of hate and a wish for vengeance, written by someone who is obviously experiencing deep anger and humiliation." The writer's imagination runs wild. He visualizes a vendetta that will not only strike at his enemy directly but will strike at his enemy's family and future as well. He wants nothing less than the total humiliation of the one who has wronged him.

"Do it to him, Lord," the writer seems to be saying, "for I am right and he is wrong, and I trust that you will show yourself to be a God who knows which side to take." But, before we address the question of whether God will do what he asks, I suppose that there is something to be said for his asking it in the first place. I suppose the psalm might be considered "therapeutic" for the writer. Perhaps, after setting his pen down, he felt better. One hopes he felt better. There is something to be said for getting things off your chest. And who better to "get it off your chest" to than God. Perhaps, suggests Brueggemann, it is an act of prayerful catharsis and unburdening of soul that will free the writer from the paralysis of anger. Maybe so. I won't argue the point.

I suppose the psalm might also strike a responsive chord among those who have felt similar rage and not known what to do with it. Perhaps you heard these words read and thought: "The psalm does not speak to me. I have never felt this angry." If that be the case, take a moment to ask yourself:

Whose psalm is it, then?

Who does it speak to?

Who has felt this angry?

If, in the course of trying to think of somebody, it helps put you in touch with the intensity of that person's pain and anger, reading the psalm will not have been in vain.

But, having said something nice about this not-very-nice piece of scripture, we still have to address the question avoided earlier. Will God honor the writer's request? Certainly, God will not refuse to hear it. But God is under no obligation to grant it. Last week, at the conclusion of my story about the young mother who longed to see the day when her child's father would rot in hell, I asked four questions:

What if God does not vindicate her by destroying him?

What if God executes justice on God's terms, not hers?

What if God "gets him for that" in a way that she never anticipated or intended?

What if God goes "soft" at the end?

He may, you know. Go soft, that is. And it will be to the chagrin of many. Was anyone ever angrier than Jonah, when God sent him to preach his best hellfire and brimstone sermon to the Ninevites and then God changed His mind and evidenced neither hellfire nor brimstone, both of which Jonah was looking forward to with no small measure of glee?

And concerning Psalm 109, Brueggemann adds, "One hopes the writer is aware that while God may avenge, it will be in God's own way and in God's own time ... and perhaps not as the writer would wish or hope. God is not a robot. God does not implement our violent yearning without passing it through His sovereign freedom, marked by majesty, mercy, and compassion."

What does that mean for the date rapist and the young lady who lives for the day when he will rot in hell? Will he? Or won't he? If he will, will she be happy? And if he won't, will she be sad? Simple questions, really. But I can't answer any of them.

Will he rot or not?

That's God's call!

Will she be happy or sad, depending on whether he rots or not?

That's her call!

Being a preacher is easy when you know which questions are yours and which are somebody else's. But I doubt that you will let me off the hook that easy. Besides, I do have a hunch or two. I think that, sooner or later, God will go soft. In other words, I'd bet against his rotting. And I think that sooner or later, God will go to work on her heart so that she won't feel too sad or disappointed when he doesn't Having said that, let me add five qualifiers and a pair of addendums. Let's start with the qualifiers.

First, I believe that the wrath of God is real. I believe God gets angry. I believe God gets good and angry (which is not a contradiction in terms). I believe God gets good and angry at date rapists. I believe God gets good and angry at Walter. I believe God gets good and angry at me. So much for those who paint God in nothing but pastel colors. The artist always needs to hold back a red crayon with which to occasionally color God's face.

Second, I believe that the judgment of God is real. I shall have more to say about this in February. Much more. God is not mocked. People who break the laws of God eventually find themselves broken upon them. It's the way the universe operates. You can look it up.

Third, I believe that the punishment of God, while not always immediate (and certainly not always apparent), has a certain inevitability about it. Nobody gets off scot-free. Choices have consequences. And bad choices tend to have bad consequences.

Fourth, I believe that some bad consequences look and feel very much like hell. And concerning hell, the question is not "Where is it?" (the location is highly personal). Neither is it "How many of us will spend some time there?" (most all of us, I suspect). The question is "Will hell get the last word over any human life?" (I doubt it.)

Fifth, I do not know if hell is a place or a condition … I do not know if hell is more frequently experienced after we die or before … I do not know if people enter hell by sentence or by choice … I do not know what people do when they find themselves in hell (do they rot there … burn there … endure eternal root canals there … or spend twenty-four hours a day listening to country music there?). Beats me! And concerning such specifics, I don't think that any of you know any more than I do. So much for my qualifiers.

Now, for my pair of addendums. First, I choose to cast my vote with that wing of the church that says that hell is probably the first place God goes looking for his friends, certainly not the last. There is that marvelous passage in First Peter 3:19-20, where it says that between the crucifixion and the resurrection, Jesus went and preached to "the spirits in prison who formerly did not obey." And, lest there be any doubt about what "spirits" in what "prison," he continues in 4:5-6 by saying that, "the Gospel was preached, even to the dead, that though judged in the flesh like men, they might live in the spirit, like God." "He descended into hell" is the way the Apostle's Creed puts it. Fred Buechner points to the irony of it all when he writes, "Christ, of all people, in hell, of all places. But, then again, why not?" Where else would he go? What else would he do? It's all very much in character, really."

Second, if hell is where God goes to look for His friends, I suspect it is also where godly Christians will go to look for their enemies. Think about it. The very qualities that are most likely to get us into heaven ... qualities like mercy, kindness, compassion, understanding, and forgiveness ... will probably not allow us to enjoy heaven, once we know that there are others who remain lost, missing, struggling, and excluded. One night, Kris and I were dinner guests at a very exclusive dining club, having been invited by a lady who both enjoyed that place and was most confident of her own. The meal was lovely, lavish in every detail. And, I won't kid you, I like such things. I really do. But midway through the meal, I was taken aback when the lady bent her head toward mine and whispered, "Not just anyone can come here, you know." She said it to make me feel special. And I had felt special until she said it. But once said, it took something of an edge off the evening. For I realized that the part of me that enjoys places where "not just anyone can come, you know" is not the best part of me. And it is certainly not the part of me that is going to qualify me for heaven.

Therefore, I figure that heaven is empty, much of the time, because all of its occupants will have signed out on mission work camps to hell, where the real work of the saints is still being done.

I am a universal salvationist. This means that I believe that somehow, by some means, in the best possible way, God'll get us all in the end. Strangely enough, near the end of his life, the old crusty Swiss theologian Karl Barth may have done a 180-degree turn and come to the same conclusion. Said Barth, in answer to a question following his last American appearance in Chicago, **"Would it really be so bad if ... at the end ... out of His infinite mercy ... God were to find a way to draw all of us to Himself?"**

That idea satisfies me. I don't know if it will satisfy my young lady friend who lives to see the father of her child rotting in hell. Strangely enough, she may get a closer look than she bargained for, given her hardness of heart. Then both of them will find themselves dependent upon the mercy of God. Along with me! And you!

October 29, 1989
Nardin Park United Methodist Church
Farmington Hills, Michigan

Note: In a later version this sermon was entitled "On Whether the Oklahoma City Bomber Should Rot in Hell." This earlier version was widely applicable to multiple situations.

Harold Kushner's book, Who Needs God? was published by Simon and Schuster in 1989.

18

WHEN THE ROLL IS CALLED UP YONDER WHO'LL BE THERE?

The church, both universal and local, splits over the question implied by this title. There are parishioners who have parted company with me upon learning where I stood on this matter. But thankfully, reading a sermon is safer than hearing a sermon. The issue being one of distance. Hopefully, we will remain friends, both presently and eternally.

Scripture: John 12:27-32, Philippians 2:1-11

Shopworn (and more than a little shaggy) is the story about the Methodist, newly arrived in heaven, being given a tour of the premises by St. Peter. Down the hallway they walk, Peter pointing out the doors. "Behind this door, the Catholics. Behind that one, the Presbyterians. And that door over there opens on the Lutherans. But when we pass this next door, we need to tiptoe very quietly." "Why is that?" the Methodist inquires.

"Well," said St. Peter, "that's where the Baptists are. And they think they're the only ones here."

Like I said, the story is as old as it is apocryphal. You could change the names, and no one would be the wiser. The only reason the story survives is because there are groups who believe they will be the only ones there ... ought to be the only ones there ... and have a God-given right to be the only ones there.

Among those certain that God is going to cap heaven's population, there seems to be a division between those who are delighted by the idea of limits and those who are worried by the idea of limits. With the greatest worry of the worriers being: "What if I'm there, and my loved ones aren't?"

Several times in my ministry (including here, recently) retired individuals in their seventies and eighties have come to me about a concern, raised by one of their children or grandchildren, that they (their grandparents) won't be going to heaven. Now mind you, these retirees have (in every instance) been lifelong members of the church ... workers in the church ... and generous givers to the church. And once upon a time ... seventy years ago when they were confirmed ... some pastor asked them, "Do you accept Jesus Christ as Lord and Savior?" To which they remembered saying, "Yes, I do."

But now, someone in their family is saying to them:

> *That may be true, Grandma and Grandpa, but there's something about that moment that wasn't right. Either the words weren't right, the mood*

wasn't right, the means weren't right, or the church (especially the church) wasn't right. Because it wasn't our church. It wasn't the right church. It wasn't the true church. So give us some assurance by doing it our way. Which, we believe to be the only way. Because heaven won't be the same without you.

Even clergy families are not immune. Steve Swecker is a fellow Methodist minister (ordained in West Virginia but now living and serving in Maine). While we have never met, we both have essays in a newly-published collection entitled Wells of Wisdom: Grandparents and Spiritual Journeys. In Steve's essay, he describes the day he became a great disappointment to his grandmother, creating a wedge in their relationship that never healed. It was the day he was ordained as a United Methodist minister. But he can tell it better than I can.

Not once did it occur to me as a young man in my twenties that my decision to seek ordination to the Methodist ministry would distress a family member, much less, Grandma. As far as I was aware, she was proud of me, and her blessing seemed secure.

It stunned me, therefore, to learn through my mother that not only was Grandma not proud of my decision to enter the ministry, but she believed my doing so would effectively cut me off from any possibility of salvation. Until my vocational decision was made, she could hope that someday I would see the light and embrace the rock-ribbed Church of Christ that had shaped her spiritual understanding since childhood. According to her church's belief, it alone possessed the gospel truth and keys to heaven. Hence, the prospect of her grandchild—her beloved Stephen—becoming an "unsaved" United Methodist preacher erected a barrier that stood between us for the rest of her life.

One of the last times I saw Grandma after crossing the spiritual Rubicon of ordination was on the front porch of my aunt's house, where Grandma was visiting at the time. Although I greeted her warmly as always, she scarcely acknowledged my presence, never looking me in the eye. It was a moment of profound sadness for me, one that some thirty-five years later still echoes in my heart.

Well, I don't know about you, but I feel the pain in that. I feel the pain in Grandma's fear. I also feel the pain in Stephen's loss (if not of heaven, then of Grandma). But I feel even greater pain when the promises of God … which are offered, I think, to bridge us together … keep wedging us apart.

Let me be both forthright and honest with you. In all my years of preaching, nothing I have said about any social issue … even the most controversial and volatile social issue … has generated as much feedback (some of a questioning nature, some of a critical nature) as my claim that God's desire is to **heal all** of his creation, **redeem all** of his children, **restore all** of his family, and **re-gather all** of his people. Meaning that heaven's population may turn out to be more numerous than many think … more diverse than many think … more inclusive than many think … and hence, more surprising than many think. Making the "church triumphant" grander and greater than many think … or want, if the truth be known.

I realize that every time I say that, it sounds like fingernails on the blackboard to some of you. For which I profoundly and humbly apologize. Profoundly, because I really don't want to hurt you. Humbly, because I could be wrong.

Some years ago … though not that many, really … Robert Schuller addressed several thousand pastors in Orlando, Florida. The group included mainline and Pentecostal pastors, fundamental and charismatic pastors. After his presentation, he agreed to field questions from the congregants. I wasn't there, but my friend and colleague Rod Wilmoth was. He describes the scene thusly:

> At that point, one of the clergy said, "Dr. Schuller, I read recently that you gave an address to a national gathering of Muslims. Why did you speak to them and what did you say?" There was something about the question that implied that a Christian would have no reason to speak to such a group.
>
> Robert Schuller, in his usual open and direct manner, said: "I was honored to speak at their

national gathering. I talked about what Muslims and Christians have in common. That, in many ways, we both come from the same roots and that we could accomplish much by working together, focusing not on our differences but on our similarities." And then, sensing the uneasiness with the question, Dr. Schuller said, "Let me tell you about a book I'm reading now. The author said, 'Don't be surprised if, when you die and go to heaven, you will meet people there who have never heard of Jesus Christ.'"

I doubt if everyone present especially liked what Dr. Schuller said, but it was the right thing to say, given where we are in our world today. Christians who feel that they have exclusive membership in heaven may be in for a real surprise. My congregation has often heard me say, "If you have Jewish neighbors and you're not getting along, you had better work on improving the relationship because, in all reality, they will be with you in heaven!"

I believe that. As does Father Richard John Neuhaus (currently the most influential Catholic scholar in America). I read Father Neuhaus because he is a most eloquent spokesperson for what might be called Christian conservatism in America. I also read him because I need to give people access to me who, on many issues, think differently from me. But concerning my broader understanding of salvation, I was surprised to discover he stands with me. His recollection of how that line of thinking began is one of the best biographical memories I have read in years.

When I was a boy, no more than seven years old, I attended a "mission festival" in the Canadian hamlet of Petawawa, Ontario. The annual mission festival was a very big event among the people of that time and place. Each parish would take its turn in hosting the mission festival, and since individual churches could not hold the crowds that came from surrounding parishes, the day of preaching, prayer, hymns and picnicking was held outdoors. For such a special occasion, a guest preacher was required, and this year he came all the way from "the States," which meant two hundred miles away in upstate New York. This preacher had a most dramatic flair in making the case for the urgency of world missions. Well into a sermon that lasted an hour or more, the preacher suddenly stopped. For a full minute, there was complete silence as he looked intently at his wristwatch. Then he tossed his head, threw out his arm and, pointing directly at me in the third row, announced: "In the last minute, thirty-seven thousand lost souls have gone to eternal damnation without a saving knowledge of their Lord and Savior Jesus Christ!"

It was, I believe, the first theological crisis of my life. This seven-year-old boy was electrified. I immediately put my mind to work figuring out how many minutes we had been sitting there while thirty-seven thousand people per minute were going to hell. I looked around and was puzzled to see everybody else taking the news so calmly. Mrs. Appler was straightening the bow in her daughter's hair, and Mr. Radke was actually smiling as he nodded approval at the preacher's words. Hadn't they heard what he said?

In my agitated state, I wanted to jump up and shout that we had better get going right now to tell all those hell-bent people about Jesus. The real crisis came later, however. I was excited all day and had spent a restless night contending with dreams about all those people in hell. The next morning I discovered that the visiting preacher and my dad (who was the pastor of the host church) were taking three days off to go fishing.

Thirty-seven thousand people going to hell every minute and they were going fishing! I knew there was something very wrong here and wrestled with the possible explanations. Maybe they didn't care about all those people. It was not only my dad and the other preacher but my mom, my brothers and sisters and the entire parish who seemed to be taking very much in stride yesterday's announcement of cosmic catastrophe. This said something not at all nice about the people who were dearest to me. Slowly, another explanation began to recommend itself. The mission festival preacher didn't really mean what he said. Not really. And everybody understood that, except me. After a time, my initial alarm subsided as I came to think that he and they did not mean it at all, that it was just "church talk" and not to be taken too seriously.

I think the question of salvation must always be taken seriously. But I have fought for forty years against its being taken narrowly. There is much in the Bible suggesting that God's desire is that all be saved. Let me illustrate with a few examples.

- I Timothy 2:4: "God desires all to be saved and come to full knowledge of the truth."

- Ephesians 1:7-10 speaks of God's purpose ... set forth in Christ ... "to unite all things in him."

- Colossians 1:15-20 suggests that the purpose of God, through the cross of Christ, is "to reconcile all things to him," whether in heaven or on earth (suggesting that heaven may also include some who still need reconciling).

- Philippians 2:5-11 suggests that it is the goal and vision that, in time, "every knee shall bow and every tongue confess that Jesus Christ is Lord, to the glory of God the Father."

- John 12:32 has Jesus saying: "And when I am lifted up, I will draw all people to myself," with common agreement suggesting that this passage intends nothing less than "universal range of atonement."

Clearly, the question of your destiny (or mine) is both very personal and very important.

Will I be saved?

Will you be saved?

Will either of us go to heaven?

Or, neither of us?

But the focus of such questions is surprisingly and shockingly individualistic ... even self-centered. The question of the gospel is not simply, "Where will I spend eternity?" The question of the gospel is, "Will God accomplish his eternal destiny?" And what is God's destiny? "That we might all be one" (the Gospel of John). "And that we might dwell in fellowship one with another" (the First Letter of John). Why? So that God's joy (and ours, for that matter) might be complete. And having seen what God desires, it should be axiomatic that God's desire be our desire.

Quoting Father Neuhaus again:

> Not only Catholics, but probably most Christians, suspect it cannot be right that the overwhelming majority of people who have ever lived will be eternally lost to the love of God. I

mean, if all the Christians in the world marshaled all the evangelistic resources in the world, and devoted twenty hours of every day to nothing but relentless proclamation of the gospel around the world, how many millions of people would still be going to hell? If this is God's plan of salvation for a world we are told he loves so much, it would seem to be seriously flawed.

Which is why the Second Vatican Council in its Gaudiam: Et Spes (*The Pastoral Constitution on the Church in the Modern World*) says:

> **We are obliged to hold that the Holy Spirit offers everyone the possibility of sharing in the cross of Christ ... in a manner known to God.**

Which allows that Jesus is still, "the way, the truth, and the life" (John 14). But, by the working of the Holy Spirit (in ways known only to the Spirit), others who have not known Christ ... who have never been introduced to Christ ... or who may have chosen other than Christ ... might yet have their ways and truths be brought into harmony with Christ. "Why?" asks Father Neuhaus. "That none may be lost." And with that statement, I am quite comfortably and fraternally Catholic.

I will be sad if many are damned. I will be sad if any are damned. Sad for them. Sad for me. But sadder still for God ... who will not get, at the end of the day, what God has desired from the beginning of the day. Hell may exist. But I pray that hell is continually in the process of being emptied. As for heaven, if granted access, I won't, so much, mind the company of those who behaved badly (in this life) as those who believed smugly (in this life). But if Jesus really is the Great Physician, then even spiritual arrogance can be healed.

Hearing me preach a similar sermon 28 years ago, an angry young mother (why is it always the young?) scalded me at the door: "If you mean I may have to spend eternity with the likes of Charles Manson, then I don't want to go." Not quite knowing what came over me ... or who came into me ... all I could think of to say was: "Gail, beggars can't be choosers."

•••••

But just in case you are wondering, I am so glad I gave my life to Jesus Christ early in my teenage years. Not because I might have died. But because I didn't.

June 5, 2005
First United Methodist Church
Birmingham, Michigan

Note: *I am aware that other New Testament passages can be cited that would appear to contradict the universality of God's desire "that all be saved." I have wrestled with those passages in previous sermons and chose not to read them into the record here. If the Bible spoke with the clarity of "one voice" on this matter, we would have less conflict in theology classes and fewer arguments in the church.*

For purposes of this sermon, I am heavily indebted to Richard John Neuhaus and his penetrating book, Death on a Friday Afternoon: Meditations on the Last Words of Jesus From the Cross. Those of a more conservative bent will find Father Neuhaus interesting, given his attempts to reconcile John 14:6 with a more universal understanding of salvation. For persons not wishing to read the entire book, a careful study of chapters two and five will unwrap the main argument.

Steve Swecker's reminiscence of his grandmother can be found in a new book entitled Wells of Wisdom: Grandparents and Spiritual Journeys (edited by Andrew Weaver and Carolyn Stapleton). Rodney Wilmoth's remembrance of Robert Schuller can be found in his book, How United Methodists Share Their Faith. And I am grateful to my friend, Jim Standiford of First United Methodist Church, San Diego, for recalling the old joke about St. Peter and the doors in heaven. Ironically, the sermon in which Jim shared this story was entitled "Full House."

19

WHY DON'T THINGS LIKE THAT EVER HAPPEN TO ANYBODY WE KNOW?

In my life I have preached nearly 50 sermons on Easter Sundays ... a few outdoors at sunrise ... but most, at a more civil hour, in a sanctuary. Once you have said something fifty times, it's not easy to be original. What follows is my last Easter sermon in 2005. It may also be the one I like best.

Scripture: I Corinthians 15:3-19

Thomas Long is a most interesting fellow who presently does full-time what I am soon to do part-time ... namely, teach divinity students a little bit about preaching. In his most recent book, *Testimony: Talking Ourselves Into Being Christian,* he reports the following:

> Recently I was driving across town at rush
> hour and scanning the radio for a traffic report

when the dial happened to pause on a Christian talk radio station. The talk show host was taking telephone calls from listeners that day, and a woman named Barbara had called in. Barbara had problems; Barbara had a lot of problems. She had problems with her boss at work. She complained about trouble in her marriage. She was at odds with her teenaged children. She said she had occasional bouts of depression.

As she unfolded her litany of troubles and woes, suddenly the talk show host interrupted her. "Barbara," he said, "I want to ask you something. Are you a believer? You know, you're never going to solve any of these problems unless you're a believer. Are you a believer?"

"I don't know," said Barbara hesitantly.

"Now, Barbara," said the host, "either you are a believer, or you aren't. If you're a believer, you know it. You know it in your heart. Barbara, tell me, are you a believer?"

"I'd like to be," Barbara replied. "I guess I'm just more agnostic at this point in my life." The talk show host reacted quickly to that. "Now Barbara, there's a book I've written that I want to send to you. In this book, I prove that Jesus was who he said he was and that he was raised from the dead.

Now, if I send you this book and you read it, will you become a believer?"

"I don't know," she said. "I've had a lot of trouble from preachers."

"We're not talking about preachers," the host said. "We're talking about proof! I've got proof, irrefutable proof, that Jesus was who he said he was and was raised from the dead. Now, if I send this book to you, will you become a believer?"

Barbara was frustrated. "I don't think you're listening to me," she said. "I'm having trouble trusting at this point in my life."

"Barbara," he said, "we're not talking about trust. We're talking about truth. I have unassailable proof. Now, if I send it to you, will you become a believer?"

"I guess so," Barbara said. "Yeah, I'll become a believer."

I only know a handful of people who would call that good evangelism. And, frankly speaking, I don't know anybody who would call that good pastoral care. If Barbara sounds far from convinced, there are understandable reasons for her skepticism. Beginning with the talk show host. Had he really heard her? What was he trying to sell her? And why had he turned the conversation so quickly from her problems to his book?

But quite apart from the personality of the host, there remains the veracity of his claim to have proof. The fact is, there isn't any. There is no scientific proof of the resurrection … no videotape of Jesus vacating the tomb … no seismograph of any Easter weekend earthquake … no first-person interviews and news at 11:00. Which is why the endless sifting of the scanty sources (which has been carried out for centuries by amateur sleuths as well as scholarly analysts) convinces no one and is always so unsatisfying. The most recent case in point being the Shroud of Turin.

What we have is testimony, not proof. Someone saw him and told someone else. Women saw him and told the story to men. Men saw him and told the story to each other. Those first to hear it were frightened. Eventually, however, the frightened became emboldened. And it was clear that the story had life-changing capability. Leading generation after generation to say: "How can it not be true, because look at all the wonderful things it has accomplished." Do not diminish the power of the testimony. I have heard it. I have read it. I have preached it. I believe it. Although I can't prove it. And, in point of fact, stopped trying to prove it 25 or 30 years ago.

Preachers, when they are young, get all caught up in the literalness of what happened. But there comes a point when the more interesting question becomes the meaning of what happened. I am talking about the movement from "what" to "so what." In today's text, Paul tells us "so what." Paul says: "If it isn't true (that Christ was raised from the dead), then we're liars. Worse yet, we are pitiable liars. And worst of all, it means that everybody else who has died is as dead as Christ is, and when we die, we shall be as dead as the entire lot of them."

Which cuts to the crux of the matter, does it not? The primary reason most of us wrestle with the resurrection of Jesus is because of the implications it may have for the resurrection of ourselves. I suppose it is possible to consider the resurrection of Jesus as something that happened one time to one man, but makes no promises concerning other times and other men (or other women, for that matter).

And I suppose it is possible to applaud that, as well as affirm that. "Yes, if anybody should be raised from the dead, it should certainly be Jesus ... good man that he was ... God's man that he was ... young man that he was ... horribly mistreated man (I mean, did you see Gibson's film?) that he was. Yes, if anybody deserves to be resurrected, Jesus deserves to be resurrected." But in forty years of Easter preaching, I've never heard anybody say that. Churches don't fill up on Easter with people who say: "I'm glad it turned out so well for him." Rather, churches fill up on Easter with people who, if pressed, will say: "I hope it will turn out so well for me." There is, at the heart of our faith, a certain selfishness. Given that most of us come to church on Easter, not so much to say, "Good for him," but, "Good for us."

Lindsey Crittenden (in an essay sufficiently well-crafted so as to be included in *The Best American Spiritual Writing for 2004*) remembers how, on the way home from her very first Easter service as a four-year-old sitting in "big church," she responded to the resurrection by saying to her mother, "Maybe someone in our family will do that." Interesting, isn't it, that as a four year old, the thing that fascinated her about the miracle was that it might be repeatable.

"Maybe someone in our family will do that."

In the small Pennsylvania town where Harvey Cox grew up, it was the tradition to gather in the park at sunrise on Easter, before heading to the church with the biggest Fellowship Hall for heaping platters of pancakes topped with ladles of maple syrup and slathered with chunks of creamery butter, with crisp bacon on the side and orange juice in waxy paper cups. After which he went home to greet his parents (who were not churchgoers) coming downstairs to breakfast in their bathrobes. It always made him feel a little self-righteous, going to worship in the dark and cold when his parents were tucked comfortably in their beds. But, at that stage in his life, it was more about the pancakes than the preaching ... more about seeing his friends in the park than seeing the truth in the sermon:

> But that all changed when I became a teenager and people I knew began dying. And the whole business became more urgent when I went to work, part-time, for my Uncle Frank who was the town's only undertaker. I went out with his crews to pick up the bodies. I watched him embalm some of them with formaldehyde on the white porcelain table. I helped people carry caskets to the cemetery. Some of the people we buried were old, some young, some stout, some thin. But to me, they all had one thing in common. They all looked very dead. Yet at the graveside, whatever minister was in charge always talked about the

resurrection of the dead. And, at that very impressionable age, it dawned on me that those ministers were not just talking about Jesus.

Or, as the little girl said, "Maybe someone in our family will do that."

So what do I believe? I believe that the resurrection is not about one of us, but all of us. But I also believe that the resurrection is God's work, not ours. Jesus did not rise from the dead. Let me repeat that: Jesus did not rise from the dead. Instead, Jesus was raised from the dead. There's a world of difference.

As much as I love the hymn we just sang, never failing to attack the chorus with great gusto ...

> *Up from the grave he arose*
> *With a mighty triumph o'er his foes,*
>
> *He arose a victor from the dark domain*
> *And he lives forever with his saints to reign.*
> *He arose. He arose. Hallelujah, Christ arose.*

... the Jesus portrayed in that hymn looks a little bit like Superman, awakening from an overdose of Kryptonite, revivified with strength, vigor, and vitality. For did we not just sing:

> *Death could not keep its prey, Jesus my Savior.*
> *He tore the bars away, Jesus my Lord.*
> *No. 322 UMC Hymnal*

We're talking Jesus as Superhero, right out of the pages of Action Comics. Meaning that you should probably go home and put a Jesus action figure in your kid's Easter basket. A fascinating image. But a terribly mis-focused one. Nowhere does it say that Jesus roused himself from death. What it says is that God raised him from death.

Why? Because justice demands it, that's why. From God's perspective, eternal life is not so much about getting us together in some beloved reunion (wonderful as that idea seems to me), but about God's getting it right ... getting it fixed ... getting it worked on, worked out and worked through ... so that what didn't work in this life can be made to work in the next. I have heard it said that the undergirding axiom of our faith is that "God is working his purpose out." But it would seem that God needs a bigger stage than this world affords, and a longer time frame than human history allows, in order to get it accomplished.

People say there is no concept of the resurrection in the Old Testament. To be politically correct, we are no longer supposed to refer to the first 66 books of the Bible as the Old Testament ... the word "old" suggesting things that are outdated, antiquated and tired. Instead, we are supposed to talk about the Hebrew Bible. But it is patently untrue to suggest that the Hebrew Bible lacks conceptualizations of resurrection. There are multiple conceptualizations of resurrection in the Hebrew Bible. To be sure, they differ as to how the dead will be raised or when the dead will be raised. But there is no disagreement as to why the dead will be raised. The dead will be raised so that God can make right what didn't go right ... healing the inequities ... vindicating the victims ... reconnecting the disconnected (what do you think Ezekiel's vision of the dry bones is all about?) ... and restoring to its essential goodness a creation gone sadly sour. Resurrection, in the Hebrew Bible, is a moral necessity, so that God who, in this life, is not able to deliver on all of his promises, gets to finish a work well-conceived but incompletely executed. For the Israelites, resurrection has less to do with our happiness than God's fulfillment.

Let me ask you some tough questions. Do you think that God designs everything that happens ... wills everything that happens ... desires that everything should happen exactly as it happens? I don't. And if you are with me in that conviction, you have no choice but to conclude that God does not like everything that happens, to the point of feeling pain (and more than occasional anger) over a lot of things that do happen. Some of which can be fixed here. But not all of which can be fixed here. Seen from the pages of the Hebrew Bible ... and from the perspective of a Jewish mindset ... Easter is simply the logical extension of another word beginning with "E" ... or another miracle beginning with "E." I am talking about the word "Exodus" ... with both Exodus and Easter being different, but highly complimentary ways in which God delivers his people.

In the wake of some beautiful things that have happened over the past weeks and months of our lives, both Kris and I have recently said ... out loud ... to each other ... that if the curtain were to ring down right now, we would have no regrets. Sure, we want to do more. But we've done plenty. Sure, we want to see more. But we've seen plenty. We don't feel we are owed anything. Nor do we feel that we have been cheated out of anything. For us, from here to wherever is largely gravy.

But every day we either run into, or read about, people who don't say that because they can't say that ... who, from the great poker hand of life, have drawn an extremely low card (would you believe the two of clubs?) ... or from the tight-fisted hand of fate have drawn an extremely short straw. Or maybe the straw they drew was long enough in the beginning ... even strong enough in the beginning ... but the randomly-swinging sickle of chance chopped it down, sliced it up, or whacked it off before it ripened into the full flavor of its promise. The fact of the matter is, some people get the shaft. Other people give the shaft. But, in the short run, it is God's dream and design that gets shafted. Resurrection, biblically considered, is less about human reward than it is about divine reconstruction ... God working his purpose out.

Which means that whether Terry Schiavo dies tomorrow or twenty years from tomorrow is really secondary. Any pleasure God takes in whether the tube stays out or goes back in ... whether her parents win or her husband wins ... whether the Religious Right wins or whether the equally-religious Left wins ... I think is minimal. Compared, that is, with the pleasure that God will take in seeing her life restored more than merely sustained. If it were me, I would hope it would happen immediately. But if it does not, I believe it will happen eventually ... and inevitably. Because God's purpose will be worked out. And because God is good.

•••••

The Resurrection:

Did it happen once?
    Yes.

Will it happen again?
    Yes.

Will it happen to anyone we know?
    Yes.

(and here's the controversial one) …
Will it happen to everyone we know?
    Yes.

Will we be universally happy if it happens to everyone we know?
    Maybe. Maybe not.

The phone rang frantically in the home of a man locally. It was a call from Israel telling him: "Your mother-in-law fell from the back of a camel while on a tour of the Holy Land and died. But I have done some checking before calling. And I can tell you that flying her home for burial will cost in the neighborhood of $15,000. But if you allow her to be buried here in the Holy Land, we can do it for $150."

Without missing a beat, the son-in-law said, "I'll wire the $15,000 tonight. Put her on the first plane tomorrow morning." "Will do," said the tour operator. "But might I ask, given the huge differential in price, why you passed on such a deal?"

To which the son-in-law said, "The last person I knew who was buried in your country was up and walking around again in three days. And I simply can't take the chance."

Well, I would love to see my mother-in-law up and walking around again. Truth be told, I would love to see my worst enemy up and walking around again. Not because of what it might say about the merits of my enemy. And not because of what it might say about the merits of me. But because of what it will say about the goodness of God. God is working his purpose out. But the only way God wins is if everybody wins.

Easter Sunday 2005
First United Methodist Church
Birmingham, Michigan

Note: *For a concise discussion of the "justice theme" of resurrection narratives in the Hebrew Bible, let me direct you to Harvey Cox's treatment of "The Easter Story" in his recent book* When Jesus Came to Harvard, *Houghton Mifflin Company, 2004. I have benefited greatly from Cox's treatment of the Holy Week themes throughout this Lenten season.*

Thomas Long taught preaching at Emory University in Atlanta. His book, Testimony: Talking Ourselves Into Being Christian, *is part of "The Practices of Faith Series," published by Jossey-Bass in 2003.*

Lindsey Crittenden's essay is entitled, "The Water Will Hold You" and can be found in The Best American Spiritual Writing, 2004 edited by Philip Zaleski.

As concerns "testimony" as the primary source of evidence for the resurrection, it is a position held by scholars of all stripes including those firmly rooted in the evangelical connection. Oxford's Richard Swinburne gives primary credit to the apostles' Easter "testimony" for the dramatic spread of the gospel. To which Notre Dame's Alvin Plantinga (whom Christianity Today magazine calls the most important philosopher of any stripe) says, "Maybe it's not knock-down, drag-out, one-hundred-percent-conclusive evidence, but it's pretty strong evidence." To which Plantinga adds another factor emphasized by Aquinas and Calvin … internal knowledge from the Holy Spirit that convinces an individual that such testimony is true.

The Terri Schiavo case captured the attention of entire nation, given that it involved both a family dispute and a national debate over what heroic measures should be used to address the issue of life's preservation.

20

THE SON'S UP

For those of you who like Easter sermons, this is your lucky day. While included in this collection, it was first written and delivered in 2004. I will probably never preach another, given that few employed preachers yield their pulpits to retirees on Easter Sunday. This sermon is somewhat unique, however, given the story about our son, Bill Ritter Jr., with which it closes.

Scriptures: Matthew 28:1-15, 1 Peter 1:3-10

Seven short days ago, exhilarated but spent after a vigorous morning of Palm-Sundaying with the likes of you, your children and your children's children, I went home for a little R and R. I went alone, given that the trophy wife I married over 37 years ago was attending a shower. The refrigerator yielded a few leftovers, and the microwave rendered them edible, so I parked both food and body in front of the telly to watch the Pistons do battle with the Pacers.

But given that basketball had not yet begun, I hit that little button on the clicker that jumps you to the channel last watched before this one. Which is how I arrived at the Travel Channel and their countdown of "The Ten Best Beaches for Tanning in the World." As I remember it, one was in Hawaii, one in Monte Carlo (all the places you might expect), although one was in Thailand (which is not a place I would have expected).

Each beach featured water and sand, sun and fun ... and flesh (lots and lots of flesh). I mean, when I turned back to the Pistons, they were covered up like the Amish in comparison to the people on those beaches. But I felt very old when my first thought about those uncovered bodies was the danger that the sun might pose for their skin forty years from now. Given that come Tuesday, some surgeon is going to dig a couple of holes in my face to repair the ravages of rays absorbed in the years when, if I wasn't too young to know better, I was certainly too young to care.

Yet all of us enjoy the sunshine. Most of us crave the sunshine. While a few of us absolutely require the sunshine. Early in my employment here, I shared leadership with a colleague who suffered from SAD (Seasonal Affective Disorder). Which was a real malady ... a winter malady ... a when-the-day-is-gray-I-feel-debilitated-and-depressed malady. So she outfitted her family room with a series of bright lights in whose glow she absolutely needed to sit for an hour or two in order to become her old self again. In a world of heat-seeking missiles, many of us are light-seeking people.

Never did I realize this so much as I did in Costa Rica where, in the span of a few days, I became learned in the subtleties that distinguish dry forests from cloud forests from rain forests. I walked over and through the tops of trees on those wonderful suspension bridges (which, depending on the elevation of the span and the velocity of the wind, were more harrowing than thrilling). But atop the forest it was light. In the forest, it was dark. So dense was the vegetation that, although it never stopped raining, I never got wet. Damp, certainly. Musty, inevitably. But wet, hardly.

As I told you a few weeks ago, I learned that over seventy percent of the plant growth in the rain forest (orchids, ferns, bromeliads) grows from the tops of the trees. All it takes is a crack in a branch for a seed to lodge and flower there. Because there is light up there, don't you see? For there to be light in the midst of the forest, a tree has to fall to the floor of the forest, cutting a swath through the heart of the forest, allowing space for the sun so as to recreate the forest.

But of greatest amazement were the walking palms. A trunk would emerge from the ground in one place, grow a foot above the ground in that place, then turn abruptly ninety degrees to the right or left (growing parallel to the ground) until launching upward at some other place. Why the jog in the growth pattern? The search for a shaft of light, don't you see? It is as if the palm tree says to itself, "Too dark here; better I should try it over there."

Easter people understand that, given that Easter is a dark-to-light story. In John, Mary Magdalene goes to the tomb "while it was still dark," while Luke says "early dawn," Matthew says "toward the dawn," and Mark says it happened "when the sun had risen." We're talking degrees of difference here. Half light. Partial light. Dawn's early light. Shades and slivers of light. We're talking about the time of the morning when some of you like to jog, and others of you like to fish.

But brightness is emerging. Meaning that darkness is receding. The friends of Jesus have made it through the night. Just as we friends of Jesus have made it through the night. There were nights we didn't think we would … didn't think we could … weren't sure we cared. But morning broke anyway.

A variation on a time-worn story finds a man on an otherwise darkened stage, illumined by a single spotlight. He is crawling on his hands and knees, searching for his keys. When a police officer offers to help, he begins by asking the man where he lost them. "Over there," the man says. "I lost them over there." Prompting the question as to why he is looking for them over here. Leading the man to answer, "Because the light's better over here."

Which makes no sense if you are looking for keys. But which makes great sense if you are looking for faith. Start where the light is. Start where the Easter light is. When many of us left this place on Thursday, it was dark in here. This morning it is light in here. Jesus has come from death to life. And we have come from darkness to light.

Obviously, this morning's sermon title contains a pun that is very much intended. "The sun's up" is a phrase that, when commonly spoken, refers to the emergence of a celestial body in the sky, some 93 million miles away.

Wake up, wake up, you sleepyhead.
Get up, get up, get out of bed.
Cheer up, cheer up, the sun is red.
Live, love, laugh and be happy.

For those of you who don't have a memory chip that is older than dirt, that lyric comes from a song entitled "When the Red, Red Robin Comes Bob, Bob, Bobbin' Along" ... suggesting that "there'll be no more sobbin' when he starts throbbin' his own sweet song."

But let's be honest, friends. Robins and sunshine, while charming in their appearing, will not put a stop to much of the world's sobbing ... not to mention the world's grieving and the world's hurting. Even if you throw in daffodils. Which is why, when we say "the Son's up" in a place like this ... on a day like this ... having just read a text like this ... we know that the word "Son" is spelled with an "o" rather than a "u." What a difference a vowel makes.

The Son of God rose from the dead. God, I wish I knew how. That's a prayer, Lord. I really do wish I knew how. I wish I knew the biology of it, the chemistry of it, along with the physiology and the physics of it.

Among others, I was critical of the diminished role given the resurrection in Mel Gibson's recreation of Jesus' passion. I would have settled for a symbolic (even a cinematic) evocation of victory, triumph, and joy. Maybe there was one. But I realize that my hungering was for a "you are there ... see it now ... we interrupt your regularly scheduled programming, taking you live to an ancient burial ground in Jerusalem" kind of reporting. In short, I wanted to see the rising ... having, for 39 years, preached the results of the rising. In terms of ...

... appearances made,

... fears conquered,

... disciples empowered,

... churches birthed.

I have researched the biblical account enough to believe it, trust it and preach it ... even though I didn't see it, and lack the tools to comprehend it or the words to explain it. As Will Willimon and Joseph Haroutunian keep reminding me, resurrection is God's doing. And God's doing is not always within the realm of my understanding. Haroutunian used to ask his graduate students at McCormick Theological Seminary: "If the town reprobate and the town saint died on the same day and were buried (side by side) in the same cemetery, and God came along and said, 'Get up,' which one would get up first?" After which he would then pause before saying: "Neither, of course. For only God raises the dead." The dead do not get up. The dead are raised up.

Resurrection is godly work. There was no "bounce-back capacity" scripted into the genetic code of Jesus. Nor is there a "bounce-back capacity" scripted into the genetic code of us. As Joanna Adams writes, "When it comes to resurrections, no cooperation is needed from any of us."

And yet I would suggest to you (this blessed Easter Sunday) that while resurrection does not require our cooperation, it invites our cooperation ... in that once we allow ourselves to accept its inevitability in the future, it might actually influence our activity in the present.

I love the language of 1 Peter 1:3-9. So much so that I have written some of it into our Calls to Worship for the past several Easters. He says that we are "born into a living hope (get that ... a living hope) through the resurrection of Jesus Christ from the dead." Then he goes on to call that resurrection nothing less than "an inheritance" ... one that is "imperishable, undefiled and unfailing." An inheritance. Just think of it. You and I are in the will. That's why some of you came today. Because you knew I was going to read the will. You also came in hopes that all the relatives ... those who feel themselves favored and those who feel themselves forgotten (even the shirttail and the no-tail relatives) ... will hear their names in the reading of the will.

Although there are some of you who fear you are not in the will ... that you are going to be among the ones cut out, left out or drummed out. It sometimes devastates people when they wind up with a smaller inheritance than they anticipated. A skewed distribution of assets can actually split a family. As it did my father's fifty years ago. It opened a wound that festered forever. It never healed. And I'm the only one left who remembers it. Which means that this side of heaven, there is nobody left who can fix it.

But what if you knew that your inheritance was assured ... that it was yours for the trusting ... yours for the claiming ... yours for the living? It might make a difference, mightn't it? If you knew there was money in the future, wouldn't it inspire confidence in the present? And if you know that there is life in the future, might it not do the same (in the present)?

Wasn't it Charles Dickens who once attended a meeting with some very stuffy bishops, arch bishops, apprentice bishops and wannabe bishops? They were going on and on about less and less, entirely without feeling. When Dickens interrupted the proceedings by saying, "I have a suggestion. Why don't we move into the Conference Room, sit around the table, hold hands and see if we can get in touch with the living."

Armed with Easter's inheritance (along with its newly-inspired confidence), that sounds like an absolutely wonderful idea ... getting in touch with the living, I mean. For when people can trust that there really is light at the end of life's tunnel, the present darkness is both endurable and addressable.

Consider the visiting school teacher whose job it was to work with children who were hospitalized for long periods, the better to keep them from falling too far behind the others in their class. In preparing the visiting teacher for her next assignment, the classroom teacher said, "We are presently studying nouns and adverbs in this young man's class, and I hope you will be able to help him." Well, when she got to the hospital, the visiting teacher was dismayed to discover that the child was in the hospital burn unit, in very serious condition, experiencing great pain. Seeing him in such obvious misery, she was embarrassed (and more than a little ashamed of herself) for putting him through such a useless exercise. But a job was a job, so she stumbled through the lesson anyway.

The next morning she returned, only to be intercepted by the floor nurse who said, "What did you do to that boy yesterday?" Before the teacher could render an apology, the nurse said, "We had all but given up on him. But since your visit yesterday, he seems to be fighting back and responding to treatment." Later, the boy himself explained that he, too, had given up hope. But it had all changed when he came to the simple realization that surely they wouldn't send a teacher to pound adverbs into the head of a kid who was dying, would they? Ah, friends, when you can glimpse a future, there is no accounting for what you can do … or bear … or believe … in the present.

Kindly allow me a personal moment in closing. Most of you know of the self-inflicted death of our son (Bill) ten years ago this spring. Many of you have heard five sermons over ten years, detailing our journey through understanding, grieving and healing. And a few of you know that those sermons (with an extended introduction) are being published in a book that will be released by Morehouse Publishing Company early this fall. Should you buy the book, you won't find anything you haven't heard before or read before … except this. The book contains a brief epilogue, which we have never shared before. Quoting from myself:

> There is one remaining story I have never shared
> in public until now. That's because it is not my
> story, but Kris's. She has been marvelous through

all of this. It is her desire that I publish this book, and that this story, at last, be told. Preaching these sermons has been one thing. Listening to them, when you are the preacher's wife and the subject's mother, is quite another. On the five Sundays when I have spoken openly about Bill's death, hers - listening to them - has been the harder lot.

But I promised you a story. Here it is. On the morning of the day we were to find out about Bill's death, Kris woke from a sound sleep before seven. For a number of weeks, both of us had slept fitfully, worried as we were about our son. He would have a good day, and we'd relax, which would be followed by a bad day, and we'd begin fretting again.

Upon awakening Tuesday, May 2, Kris said she had just had the most wonderful dream. In it, Bill was happy, bubbly, confident and vibrant ... looking like his old self again ... laughing, joking, doing all of his funny impressions. In the dream, he said to her, "I know you have been worried about me. But you don't have to worry anymore. Everything is all right now. Things are great now. I'm going to be fine now, Mom, it's okay." Little did Kris know that at the time she dreamed that dream, Bill had been dead for several hours.

How do we explain that? We can't. How do we understand that? We don't. How do we treat that?

As a gift - for which we are grateful.

You never know when Easter … its wonderful promise and its buoyant hope … is going to come to you. You just never know.

April 11, 2004, Easter Sunday
First United Methodist Church
Birmingham, Michigan

Note: *The above-quoted epilogue appeared in my book, Take the Dimness of My Soul Away, published in 2004.*

I am also indebted to essays entitled "Preaching the Easter Texts: Resurrection and Vocation" by William Willimon and "Good News Indeed" by Joanna Adams. Both can be found in the Easter 2004 issue of Journal for Preachers published in Decatur, Georgia.

The song, When The Red, Red Robin Comes Bob, Bob, Bobbin Along, was written and composed by Harry Wood in 1926. It eventually became the signature song of Lillian Roth.

21

PRESENT AND ACCOUNTED FOR

This sermon, which brings my book to an appropriate ending, talks about those warriors who once "fought the good fight" and have already, "gone over the hill." It was preached at the Memorial Service of the Detroit Annual Conference of United Methodists, convened at Adrian College in June of 2005. The listing of names with which it closes is highly personal and testifies to colleagues in the ministry to whom I owe deep gratitude. When adapting this sermon for a local congregation, I have always substituted names known by others in that fellowship.

Scripture: Hebrews 11:32-39, 12:1-2

It was a Saturday much like this one, albeit thirty years ago. The place was the Methodist Theological School in Ohio where I was a trustee in those days. Given its setting on the banks of a meandering river, the graduation exercises were held out of doors on the lush green quadrangle. The library formed the background. The platform was elevated for the seating of the dominant players. Everybody else sat in folding chairs, grouped on the grass. The graduates were robed in black. The choir in white. The faculty and trustees, in every color of the rainbow ... bedecked like peacocks. And seated to the rear of this robed army were the plainclothes people. The wives of the male graduates. The husbands of the female graduates. The children of the older graduates. And the parents of the younger graduates. And seated in the very back, there were parishioners from a number of rural Methodist churches in mid-Ohio. Three years previous, those churches had taken these would-be preachers under their wings ... had loved them ... fed them ... nurtured them ... and somehow endured their "greenness." Now that these student preachers actually knew something ... and would momentarily have degrees to prove it ... they would leave for more fertile fields.

On this particular occasion, the speakers were eloquent. The dean was eloquent. The president was eloquent. The visiting dignitary (chosen to deliver the commencement address) was eloquent. But there was one who was less eloquent. That's because he was scared stiff. He was the only student on the platform, chosen to speak on behalf of the graduating seniors. As he approached the microphone, he did things that every nervous speaker does. He played with his glasses. He played with his tie. He played with the microphone. He cleared his throat. Several times. Then he spoke. And this is what he said:

> The chairs on which we sit are not the chairs of the prophets and the apostles.

The chairs on which we sit are not the chairs at the left hand of power or the right hand of glory.

The chairs on which we sit are not the chairs of the last (or even the next-to-last) judgment.

The chairs on which we sit are the property of the Greater Columbus, Ohio Rent-All Society.

Indeed they were. The chairs had been trucked in that morning. And they would be trucked out that night. Had we folded our chairs and looked on the underside of the seat, we would have seen the name of the rental company burned into the surface. The student's point was a simple one. He was saying: "Seminary is a rented chair. Wonderful as it has been ... we can't stay here. Somebody else needs our place. And greater fields of service need us. We gotta be movin' on.

But the student was making a broader point than he knew. Which I caught ... pondered ... and held for future reference. Life, itself, is a rented chair. We can't stay here, either. We can get comfortable in the chair ... repaint the chair ... rebuild the chair ... restore the chair ... refurbish the chair ... reupholster the chair ... or reposition the chair in the great living room of life. If we are wealthy enough, we can endow the chair. If I have a million dollars to spare, some university will gladly establish the "Ritter Chair of Religious Rhetoric." But I, myself, cannot occupy my endowment forever. I have to give it up and leave it behind. Life is a rented chair.

"What did you expect?" says the letter to the Hebrews. "This is not your home. You are just passing through." What did he call us? You know what he called us. He called us "strangers and exiles upon the earth." In the ultimate scheme of things, "we ain't got long to stay here." My eminent and imminent successor, Jack Harnish (in whom I take great delight), says, "With each passing year, this Memorial Service is Annual Conference for me." Knowing that the step that follows being retired is being remembered, I know the feeling. Pasture today. Heaven tomorrow. But far from finished, I suspect ... even then.

Many of you remember Archbishop Romero. He lived and served in El Salvador during the great "trouble" in the country. It was strife so pervasive that it allowed no one the privilege of neutrality. The revolution in El Salvador politicized everybody, even Catholic priests. Some would say "especially Catholic priests." Every time I complain about the trials of my profession, I think of people like Archbishop Romero. And I recognize that while it is never easy to preach anywhere, there are some places where it is a whole lot harder to preach than others.

Preaching in some places can get you killed. Which was what happened to Romero. He was martyred. Murdered. Brutally executed. And his martyrdom was different only because of his visibility. Because we knew of him in life, we heard of him in death.

I am told that on the day of his funeral, there was a great Requiem Mass in the Cathedral of San Salvador. The place was packed with people sympathetic to the cause. Together they sang the hymns, prayed the prayers, chanted the liturgies and partook of the Eucharist. But something else happened in that mass, which went on to become a custom each time a priest or nun was sacrificed to the conflict. The celebrant began to read the names … slowly … one at a time … of all the "religious" who had been killed in the great revolution. And after each name was read, a pocket of worshipers in the great congregation would cry out, "Presente," meaning just what it implies … present … here … accounted for … still with us in the struggle. One name after another was read. One shout after another was heard. "Ramirez … Presente." "Ramos … Presente." "Rivera … Presente." And then the last name, which was followed by the loudest shout of all: "Romero … Presente." The communion of the saints!

That shouldn't seem strange to you. Think back to your childhood. Go back to grade school. Your regular teacher was sick. They called in a substitute. Sometimes the substitute was an experienced pro. You couldn't rattle her. She was wise to every trick. Cunning like a fox, hair tightly coiled in a bun, flat shoes fully laced, she'd seen it all. She knew she would be tested. And she was ready.

But other times you got a green one … fresh out of sub school … unsure of herself. You could smell her fear the minute she entered the room. You knew you could test her, rattle her, confuse and confound her. While you might not be able to drive her screaming from the classroom, you could certainly delay doing much work that day. And so you started pushing her buttons when she commenced calling the roll. Class book in hand, she starts down the list of names. "Adams … here." "Bowers … here." "Carpenter … here." "Dillenburger … here." And on it goes. Twenty-six names called. Twenty-six children identify themselves as being "here." But wait. She counts the heads. There are only twenty-two heads in the room. Back to the class book. One more time through the list. Twenty-six names called. Twenty-six voices answer "here." Twenty-six children marked present. She counts heads again. There are still only twenty-two. Giggles abound. Finally, she decides to call the roll from the seating chart rather than from the class book. She finds the four vacant desks. Now she knows. But you had her going for a while.

Four children were absent that day. They were not present in body or in spirit. But on that day in the great cathedral of San Salvador, when the celebrant of the mass read the names of the martyrs and the people cried, "Presente," they were playing no joke on an inexperienced liturgist. Those persons were present and accounted for. They were there in death, every bit as much as they had been there in life ... one in the struggle ... one in faith ... one in the Lord ... "friends on earth and friends above" (as the hymn says). It was the communion of the saints.

How can this be? Darned if I know. But enough people have experienced it ... and enough people have felt it ... so as to convince me that it is something more than wishful thinking or poetic imagination at work.

Frederick Buechner ... novelist ... theologian ... masterful sculptor with words ... is one of my all-time favorite writers. He speaks of the same experience, putting it this way:

"I remember the first time I went to the great Palace of Versailles outside Paris, and how, as I wandered among all those gardens and statues, I had a sense that the place was alive with ghosts which I was barely unable to see. Sometimes, just beneath the surface of all that was going on around me, the past was going on around me, too, with such reality and such poignancy that I had to tell somebody else about it, if only to reassure myself that I wasn't losing my mind."

I've had experiences like that. I've been places where it almost seemed as if you could "fold back the air like a curtain" and the past would enter in and become one with the present … and the people of the past would enter and become one with the people of the present … so that, after a while, you couldn't tell where the past ended and the present began.

The dead make their witness! That's what our text of the evening affirms. The author details the legacy left by past heroes and heroines of the faith. He details it name by name … contribution by contribution … trial by trial … victory by victory … and, most importantly (lest the poor reader think that keeping the faith was all "ups" and no "downs"), he details it defeat by defeat. He even apologizes because he lacks the time and space to tell more stories in his litany of the faithful.

And then comes the clincher: "Wherefore we are surrounded by so great a cloud of witnesses, let us lay aside every weight, every sin, every encumbrance that clings to us like a barnacle on a ship's bottom or a burr on a saddle, so that we might better run the race that is set before us, looking to Jesus … the pioneer and perfector of our faith." What language! What an image!

The cloud of witnesses. We need them. Why? Because the

powers that are aligned against us are too much for us. When the Apostle Paul talks about the powers, the principalities and the hosts of wickedness in high places (all of which are metaphors used to describe the magnitude of the evils against which we contend), we know what he is talking about. And sometimes it seems as if we come to the battle woefully under-armed, undernourished, undermanned, (and under-womaned). Which leads my British hero, Colin Morris, to conclude:

> For such a battle, the militant church requires more allies than it can muster in any one place or at any one time.

> But it has them in the church triumphant. We must not, in assessing our strength, forget to count those regiments camped over the hill. So, before we dismiss our numbers as paltry and our faith as weak, we would do well to wait until the whole army is assembled.

What an image! The regiment camped over the hill, ready to share in the fight … comes to our aid … and tilts the odds more favorably toward our side. If this be true, it means that when we sing of the "company of heaven," the word "company" has an entirely new image. The "company" of which we speak is not so much a convivial gathering of like-minded people enjoying Happy Hour in high places, so much as a company of combatants … a battalion of those who, having fought one good fight, is now ready to take on another.

And why, pray tell, would they want to do that? Why would our struggles concern them? Why would they give a passing thought to our sorry plight? The author of the Letter to the Hebrews addresses that question, too. Because he suggests, "they did not receive what was promised and, apart from us, they shall not be made perfect."

What does this mean? Does it mean that God is a stern parent, withholding whatever reward may come to the faithful until all have died, so that all might receive it together? This would equate God with the parent who looks around the dinner table, counts heads, finds a couple of heads missing, and promptly sends the dessert back to the kitchen, saying, "There will be no cake for anybody until there is cake for everybody." No, that misses the point. That's not it at all. The dead need us for a very different reason. They need us to make their joy complete. Why? Because they didn't get the job done. They didn't get to see the work finished. They didn't get to see the promises fulfilled. They didn't get to see the Kingdom made manifest. "They all died in faith," says the author of Hebrews, "not having tasted victory."

To be sure, they had a good time. They did good work. They left a good witness. And they occasionally sipped the sweet nectar of triumph on a few lesser fronts. But even the most celebrated of them still died, never having tasted the victory the Gospel told us we were supposed to long for.

- They never saw justice roll down like water and righteousness like an ever-flowing stream.

- They never saw the lion and the lamb lying down together, with all the nations ... I mean *all* the nations ...

ascending the mountain of the Lord.

• They never saw swords and shields laid down by the riverside, while the people collectively declared: "We ain't gonna study war no more."

• They never saw the kingdoms of this world permeated by ... and blended into ... the Kingdom of our Lord and Savior Jesus Christ.

• They never saw the valley exalted, the highway straightened and the rough places made plain.

• They never saw a day when the blessings of God ... lavished abundantly on some of us ... came to be sweetly and generously shared with the rest of us.

• And they never saw the glory of the Lord revealed in such a way so that poor flesh/rich flesh ... black flesh/white flesh ... young flesh/old flesh ... gay flesh/straight flesh ... broken flesh/whole flesh ... evangelical flesh/liberal flesh ... Detroit flesh/West Michigan flesh ... might see it together.

That is why they need us so desperately. That is why they are the regiment camped over the hill. That is why the ghosts are alive in this room and the present moment trembles with the "presences" of yesterday. And that is why the favorite hymn in heaven is "When the Roll is Called Down Under, I'll Be There."

So indulge me as I call my own selected version of the roll.

·····

Note: *At the end of the sermon, I called the names of several clergy from my personal memory bank. Some died more than fifty years ago. One of them died scarcely fifty days ago. But they impacted my life once and sustain me in the struggle now. The list was highly personal and far from inclusive. But following each name, an ever-increasing chorus of voices was heard to respond, "Presente." The names included:*

Edsel Ammons	Bob Brubaker
Henry Hitt Crane	Bob Horton
Elsie Johns	David Jordan
Gary Kellerman	Ray Lamb
Dwight Loder	Orville McKay
Bill Mercer	John Mulder
Verner Mumbulo	Wayne North
John Parrish	Marshall Reed
Jim Wright	Fred Vosburg

Were I to deliver an updated version of it, today, 2018, I would feel compelled to add):

Jesse DeWitt	Ed Duncan
Terry Gladstone	Ralph Janka
Dan Krichbaum	Bill Quick
Bob Selberg	

Note, also, the relative scarcity of women clergy in the above listing. That is simply because most of the women I have admired as professional colleagues are still alive. When I began my ministry in 1965, the United Methodist clergy in the Detroit Annual Conference were virtually all males.

The wonderful quote about the regimen camped over the hill can be found in a book by Colin Morris entitled, The Hammer of The Lord, Abington Press, 1973.

Left to right: Bill Ritter, Mel Rookus, Fred Timpner, Al Fletcher
preparing to tee off in Northern Michigan.

Golfing with Brent Slay at Old Preswick in Scotland.

Bill joins this happy group of Birmingham First golfers, including Gary Valade, Zeno Windley, and Ed Adams at Sea Island, Georgia.

It was on the outing shown above that Gary Valade had a rather memorable encounter with a gator.

Jacob's first visit to a PGA Tournament was an early one.

Other Books by William A. Ritter

Preaching In The Key of Life

It has been said that the best preachers, when they craft their sermons, begin with a thoughtful analysis about what needs to be said, the scripture in which it is wrapped, and then "open a vein and bleed a little". If great preaching comes from great self-exploration and willingness to share where you are, then there should be no doubt why the sermons featured in "Preaching in the Key of Life" quickly became favorites of the faithful. Dr. William Ritter takes on a tour of some of the peaks, valleys, pauses and progressions, of his own life, and in doing so, teaches us a bit about ours. These sermons mark universal milestones of life including baptism, confirmation, graduation, marriage, death, and more, offering timeless perspectives on the life markers that we all share. Following his local church ministry at First United Methodist Church in Birmingham, Michigan (a 3200 member congregation), Ritter joined the faculty at Duke Divinity School, teaching sermon design and delivery to a new generation of church leaders. A graduate of Albion College and Yale Divinity School, Ritter is now retired and lives in Northville, Michigan with his wife, Kristine, and just across the backyard from his grandchildren. In other words, he is enjoying a very sweet key of life. *Amazon 2017 (ISBN-13: 978-197598233)*

Take The Dimness of My Soul Away: Healing After a Loved One's Suicide

In 1994 William Ritter's adult son committed suicide, sending Ritter and his family on a journey no family wants to take. Part of Ritter's own process of healing the loss of his son was to preach about it occasionally from the pulpit. This book is a collection of the sermons he preached, the first one just three weeks after his son's death, and the final one nine years later. Through them, we get a glimpse of a father and a family struggling honestly with their pain and gradually - over the years - coming to grips with their loss. Take the Dimness of My Soul Away will be a welcome companion to anyone who has lost a loved one to suicide, as well as to pastors and counselors who work with those who are grieving. Ritter offers no easy solutions, no rosy pictures, and no silver linings, but speaks honestly instead about the difficult emotions and confusion of this kind of loss, and ultimately, about a sense of hopefulness for the survivors of suicide. *Morehouse Publishing 2004 (ISBN0819221049)*

Prayers for Albion College

On these pages you will find prayers that reflect the College and the world as inextricably intertwined. These are prayers that reflect the eddies in the stream that is the maturation of young people. At the same time, they deny the myth of the Ivory Tower since they are a testimony to the oneness of "college life" and "real life." *Albion College Publishing 1996 (ASIN: B0006QLTUS)*

A FEW MORE WORDS
OF PRAISE ...

Some thirty years ago I met Bill Ritter. He put me on his sermon mailing list. As I read his sermons it became obvious that Bill was an unusually gifted preacher. His sermons were often poetic. His insights got to people where they lived. Earlier in my ministry, I had a layman who commented on my sermons every Sunday. On some Sundays, he would say "Rev, you put the hay down to where the goats could get it today."

Back in those days Bill printed his sermons on colored paper. After reading his sermons I would make copies and give the original copy on colored paper to my friend who evaluated my sermon each Sunday. Somewhere along the way there were no Ritter sermons for months. My friend who got the colored paper copies came to me one Sunday and asked, "What happened to the preacher who preaches Technicolor sermons?" That was an apt description of the Ritter sermons, which brought color, light and insight to the pulpit. Then as in this book "On Playing the Back Nine" Bill Ritter preaches sermons that strike at the heart of human need. He puts the hay down where the goats can get it.

When you read Bill Ritter, you get the feeling he has been reading your emotional email. There is not adequate room here to give an exhaustive list of the characteristics of a well-prepared sermon. One is the use of short, pithy illustrations rather than long complicated stories that are difficult to follow. There is an illustration of this in the sermon "Should I Live to be a Hundred" (page 49). This story is about the Baptism of King Aengus by St. Patrick. During the Baptism, St Patrick leaned on his sharp pointed staff and inadvertently stabbed the King's foot. After the Baptism, Patrick looked down at all the blood. Realizing what he had done he begged the King's forgiveness. "Why did you suffer in silence?" said Patrick to his King. The King replied, "I thought it was part of the ritual." The story is told with an economy of words, which makes it a powerful illustration. Each sermon in the collection gives strength to the theme "On Playing the Back Nine". There is an inherent consciousness at every age and stage of life that no one lives forever, which was expressed so well by Andrew Marvell when he wrote, "But at my back I always hear time's winged chariot hurrying near." All along the Journey, whether you are teeing off or near the end of the game, there is an awareness that "the back nine" is there.

The Rev. Thomas Lane Butts
Author and Civil Rights Advocate
Pastor Emeritus of First United Methodist Church
Monroeville, Alabama

•••••

Perhaps it does take a whole village to raise a child; however, a man of deep faith, firm convictions, love for humanity and brilliant command of language can, does, and will reinforce and even change the reader's perspective on life, death, doubt, betrayal, regret, vengeance, compromise, resurrection, forgiveness.

Dr. Bill Ritter, whose resounding voice has filled churches, cathedrals, chapels for decades, has collected twenty-one riveting sermons in a book he entitles ON PLAYING THE BACK NINE. Reverend Bill articulates with caution and passion, incredible honesty and directness, weaving Biblical texts with people's stories, old legends, church hymns, his own interpretations and perspectives in twenty-one sermons on a variety of topics he has preached over a span of 40 years.

As I read Bill's book, I laughed, I cried, I raised my fist and shouted, "Yes!" I wanted to find Bill and hug him for, as he calls it, "connectivity." His ideas, explanations, examples, interpretations caused me to reflect, consider, evaluate.

Bill writes "God loves us in our particularity" and "the only way to bear burdens is to share them" and "heaven is empty much of the time because all of its occupants will have signed out on mission work camps to hell." Amazing!

Beverly Hannett-Price
English Faculty/Detroit Country Day School

•••••

If you want to treat your mind and your soul to a rich delicacy of wit, wisdom and human experience, read Bill Ritter's wonderful book, The Back Nine. His use of metaphor, story and pithy punch line is an accumulation of decades of evaluated experience in spiritual thought, writing, ministry, and speaking. Once I got started, I could not put the book away

Scott Wilkinson
Doctor of Ophthalmology, Composer, and Lyricist

Cover photo taken by Zeno Windley on the course at Birmingham Country Club, Birmingham, Michigan. B.C.C. has been Bill and Kris' home course and the setting for many memorable occasions for over twenty years.

ABOUT THE AUTHOR ...

William A. Ritter retired on June 30, 2005 after 40 years as a United Methodist minister and 12 years as senior minister of the 3200 member First United Methodist Church of Birmingham, Michigan. Dr. Ritter's pastoral assignments have included Birmingham First (1993-2005), Nardin Park United Methodist Church, Farmington Hills, MI (1980-1993), Newburg United Methodist Church in Livonia, MI (1969-1980), and Dearborn First United Methodist Church, Dearborn, MI (1965-1969). A Detroit native, Bill was a member of Westlawn United Methodist Church. He graduated from Mackenzie High School, Detroit, MI (1958), Albion College, Albion, MI (BA, 1962) and Yale Divinity School (M.Div., 1965). Albion College awarded him an honorary DD in 1981. Bill has served on a number of denominational boards and community agencies, and was a Trustee of Albion College for 33 years.

After retirement, Bill held the title of Visiting Faculty in Preaching at Duke Divinity School, Durham, North Carolina, where he also taught church stewardship and fund-raising. He was designated Visiting Scholar in the Gerald R. Ford Institute of Public Policy and the Carl Gerstacker Institute of Professional Management at Albion College (Winter/Spring, 2006) and has taught at Ecumenical Theological Seminary in Detroit, MI. Additional post-retirement responsibilities included a mentoring program linking him with clergy in their first decade of ministry and numerous interim ministerial assignments. He served as the Executive Director of the United Methodist Union of Greater Detroit from 2009-2015.

Made in the USA
Middletown, DE
26 July 2021